THE BLACK CAT
A PLAY IN THREE ACTS

MORE WILDSIDE CLASSICS

THE BLACK CAT
A PLAY IN THREE ACTS

JOHN TODHUNTER

WILDSIDE PRESS

THE BLACK CAT: A PLAY IN THREE ACTS

This edition published 2005 by Wildside Press, LLC.
www.wildsidepress.com

PREFACE.

Mr. Grein has asked me to write a preface to *The Black Cat*. I cannot myself see much occasion for this. Why should an author be called upon to make a speech before the curtain? Because, I presume, people want to have something to talk about besides the play itself, and an author must surely have "views." Well, it is a day of views—and of talk.

The Black Cat was produced at the Opera Comique on December 8th, 1893, at one of the Independent Theatre Society's performances. It had a certain *succès d'estime* before a special audience, for whom, however, it was not written; and it has not been performed since.

The critics were wonderfully kind. They actually praised the play; some reluctantly, some with a reckless enthusiasm which quite astonished me. I had expected a much less pleasant reception.

The main objection they made to the thing was that it had a tragic ending, which they kindly suggested I had tacked on to my comedy, to appeal to the morbid taste of an "Independent" audience. Unfortunately I had done nothing of the kind. The play was conceived before the Independent Theatre had come into existence. The end was foreseen from the beginning; the tragedy being implicit in the subject. The tragic motive lay deeper than the death of the heroine, who might have been allowed to live, if that last symbolic pageantry had not had its dramatic fitness. Given the characters and the circumstances, the end is the absolutely right one.

Of course the circumstances might have been altered, and a sort of reconciliation patched up between husband and wife. But this would be a somewhat flat piece of cynicism, only justifiable on the ground taken by the *Telegraph*, that modern actors cannot play, and ought not to be expected to play, modern tragedy.

The conventional "happy ending" demanded by sentimental critics to suit the taste of sentimental playgoers, the divided parents left weeping in each other's arms over the recovered child, would also be quite possible. But surely even a modern dramatist may for once be allowed to preserve a grain of respect for nature and dramatic art? This would be an outrage against both. It would not be decent comedy, it would be mere burlesque, as sentimentality always is to the judicious.

The only other alternative I see is the exodus of the wife, with or without her child; or of the husband, with or without his mis-

tress. But this would be rank Ibsenism, and outrage British morality, which would be still more dreadful. Only a "practical
dramatist" could cut the Gordian knot, and at the last moment
introduce the erring Mrs. Tremaine, still charming in the garb of a
Sister of Mercy, to bring down the curtain upon a tableau of
Woman returning to her Duty, and Man to his Morality. And I,
alas! am not a "practical dramatist."

Still, if the play had been an experiment, I might have further
experimented with it, and rehandled its ending. But it was not in
its main lines an experiment. It was a thing seen and felt; and so it
must remain, in its printed form, at least—"a poor thing," it may
be, "but mine own!"

After the performance, came the managers, wanting to see the
play, and asking why I had not shown it to them before. Well, it
never occurred to me that any of them would seriously have con-
sidered the production of a piece so far off the ordinary lines.
They had not, like the enterprising Director of the Independent
Theatre, undertaken the dreadful trade of educating the public.
As a matter of fact, they fought shy of a piece in which "the new
hysteria" was studied, and which ended badly, or at least sadly.

A Comedy of Sighs, produced at the Avenue last spring, was
really an experiment on the taste of the British public. I wished to
ascertain whether a play depending for its interest rather upon
character and dialogue than upon plot and sensational situations,
would be at first tolerated and afterwards enjoyed by an average
audience. Perhaps the experiment was too audaciously conceived,
and too carelessly conducted, by both author and management. It
was unfortunately vitiated by the presence of a prevalent bacillus,
the British bugbear, in the test-tubes.

The new play was received with inarticulate cries of horror by
the critics. The Telegraph and the World, which had presided in
auspicious opposition over the birth of The Black Cat, now hung
terrific in unnatural conjunction in the horoscope of A Comedy
of Sighs. Here was Ibsenism again—nay, worse than Ibsenism,
Dodoism, Sarah-Grandism, Keynotism, rampant on the English
stage! For had I not most impudently exhibited The Modern Woman upon it? And although there was no tragedy this time, but
beautiful reconciliation, and return to her Duty at the fall of the
curtain, was she not there, the Abomination of Desolation?

Now we know that the Modern Woman ought not to exist
anywhere, therefore she does not exist, therefore she must be
stamped out. Mrs. Grundy and others have already begun the
good work, and have been diligently stamping her out ever since;

with such success that we may hope she will disappear, with infidelity, Ibsenism, the struggle for existence, and other such objectionable things. Meanwhile she has made her *début*, and may cry: *J'y suis, j'y reste!*

The *Comedy of Sighs* was slain, waving its tiny flag in the van of a forlorn hope; and over its dead body "Arms and the Man," its machine-guns volleying pellets of satire, marched to victory.

I do not solace myself with that belief, so comforting to the unsuccessful, that a play fails merely because of its goodness, or succeeds merely because it is bad; yet it is evident, I think, that other things besides its merits or demerits as a piece of dramatic writing may turn the scale for or against it. *A Comedy of Sighs*, with its somewhat "impressionist" sketches of character, and aberrations from the ordinary type of a "well-made play," proved to be "too lightly tempered for so loud a wind" as blows upon British bugbears—"Modern Women," and the like.

And now may I say a few words with regard to some misconceptions on the part of the critics as to my aim in writing these two plays? One of them, an enthusiast himself, did me the honour to hail me as a brother enthusiast, albeit an erring one. Possibly I am. But I have not been trying to educate the public, which is being educated past its old standards day by day, without such philanthropic effort on my part. I have not been trying to write "literary" plays. I quite agree with those who think that a play must be a play first. If it be "literature" afterwards, that is an added grace which gives it a permanent value. If it be not, still it may be a good play in its day and generation. I have not, for the sake of being unconventional, deliberately set myself to violate all the received canons of dramatic art, as practised by the "practical dramatist," thus making a convention of unconventionality. Unconventional art is impossible, and the drama, like other arts, has its conventions. But conventions change, and new ones are evolved, as new problems in art and other things—even morality itself—come in with each new tide of the human imagination. The "well-made play" of the day before yesterday is not a canon for all time, even for the most conservative playgoer.

No, what I have been trying to do is simply to write a good play. Ah yes! But what *is* a good play? The enthusiastic critic has a ready answer: "The play that succeeds, that has a long run, that has money in it!" I accept the answer for what it is worth. This potentiality of money is, like "literature," an added grace: and it certainly, in a sense, marks the survival of the fittest. But there are other standards in the great workshop of the artist, Nature. Even the plant or play that lives but a short time may cast its seed into the soil, or imagination, of its day, and, like Banquo, beget a royal race, though not itself a king.

Now, how does such a play as *The Black Cat* differ from those we see succeeding on the stage every day? Really not so very much, after all. It merely accentuates a growing tendency in the plays of the period to get more of the stuff of life, our every-day human life, typically upon the stage; with less of the traditional theatrical-academic element. The "well-made play" has itself undergone evolution since the days when it was an aphorism that not what is said but what is done on the stage is the essential thing. This of course is at once true and false, like every other truism. Without action there can be no play; and a play may be made fairly intelligible without a single spoken word, just as a scene from history or fiction may be quite recognisably depicted in a few symbolic lines, dots, and dashes, though no single human figure be decently drawn.

We must not, however, forget that action itself is language. What is called the action of a play is simply a story told by the movements of the players. But when we see a man stabbed, or a woman kissed, our curiosity is excited. We want to know something more about the people whose actions we see. This, indeed, may be roughly told by gesture and facial expression, which are themselves language; but, finally, to understand more than the barest outline of the story, we are forced to demand words. And the more we are interested in human nature the more we want to understand the thoughts, emotions, motives, characters, of the personages in action before us. Hence by gradual steps have come our latest attempts at studies of complex characters, in their struggle to solve the problems of life; or what are objected to as "problem plays." Well, why object? Every play, from *Charley's Aunt* to *Hamlet*, is a problem play. It is merely a matter of degree. Every play deals with the struggle of men and women to solve some problem of life, great or small: to outwit evil fortune. It may be merely to persuade a couple of pretty girls to stay to luncheon in your college rooms, when their chaperon has not turned up. It may be something more important.

The more interest the public and the dramatist take in human nature—that is to say, the better developed they are as regards dramatic sympathy—the more, rich, vivid, and subtle will be the play of character and passion, in the drama demanded and produced. In a word, the less wooden-pated and wooden-hearted they become, the less mechanical and commonplace will their drama be.

We are slowly emerging from the puppet-show conception of drama. Our dramatists are beginning to do more than refurbish the old puppets, and move them about the stage according to the rules of the "well-made" play. They are not content, like their predecessors, to leave their characters quite at the mercy of the actor who, in "creating" them, gave them whatever small resemblance to humanity they may have possessed. And as the play gains in vitality, the playwright begins to feel the absolute necessity for writing decent dialogue—not mere stage dialect that may be scamped and ranted *ad libitum* by the "star" to suit his own taste, or want of it, but real dialogue, which, while ideally reflecting the colloquial language of the day, taxes the intelligence and feeling of the actor to deliver properly.

This means real progress; for the dialogue is the very life of the play. It alone can bring out the essential import of the situation, the relation of character to character, at any given moment. An action, an incident, may have a thousand different shades of meaning or motive. Language, tone, and gesture give it its precise value. Plot and situations are at best but the skeleton; character and emotion are the flesh and blood. The treatment is everything.

We still want more of life, of the vital movements of our own time, upon the stage; and we shall get it by degrees. Sentimental melodrama, with its male puppet, who is hero or villain, its female puppet, who is angel or devil, may still continue to flourish among us; for it still satisfies the natural craving for romance, ideality, which the drama is bound to supply. But these things belong to a decaying phase of romance; and our so-called realism is but the first wave of a new romantic movement, on the stage as elsewhere. For when the old ideals become decrepit, we must go back to nature to get the stuff wherewith to make new ones.

As our dramatists advance with the times, people begin to go to the theatre to see plays, and not merely an actor in a part. The "well-made play," which was a piece of mechanical contrivance into which the puppets were ingeniously fitted, may some day develop into a work of art—a thing born rather than made—growing up like a flower in the imagination of the dramatist.

When that day comes, the actor, who used to "create" the part, will have to be content to let the part create him. The play will make the actor, not the actor the play; to the great benefit of both play and actor.

But why be so serious over an art whose end is only to amuse? To amuse? Yes; but we are not all equally amused by the same things. There may be forms of humour which tickle some people more exquisitely than even that magnificent making of tea in an old gentleman's hat, which convulses the *Charley's Aunt* audience. And if amusement be the object of the drama, we must take the word in an extended sense. I should myself roughly define a good play as one that, when adequately performed, can hold the attention of an unprejudiced audience from beginning to end, whether it amuses or merely interests them. It does not follow that because it may shock, or even bore, some worthy people it is a bad play. Even farcical comedy bores some people, with whom I cannot sympathise.

And now, if I have been rather hard upon the "well-made play," it must not be assumed that it is because I do not value construction. I do value it. But it should be vital, not academic, organic, not mechanical. Still, even mechanical construction is better than none at all. A play without plot is invertebrate, without bones. It is at his peril that a dramatist departs from accepted rules, even those respecting "strong" curtains and "strong" exits, though in certain cases weak curtains and weak exits may be more really dramatic. Then, valuable as dialogue is, it may be redundant, and make a play "flabby." The actor's rule, that all talk that does not carry on the action is bad, is worthy of all due respect. "You literary fellows want to say everything twice over," was the shrewd criticism of a stage-manager in a certain case. But an actor is often so absorbed in his own part that he does not easily estimate the bearing of any given speech, even his own, upon the whole play. "Cuts" at rehearsal are not unfrequently found to be too hastily made. Then, what is the action? Not merely the external incidents, but the shifting phases of thought, emotion, character, in the *dramatis personæ*. It is these that give the incidents their value, and so give dramatic interest to the plot, or story. The dialogue and the incidents are but two phases of the presentment of the story. The action may be rapid or slow, direct, or with episodes. All depends upon the treatment; and the play that one audience finds detestable may delight another.

If *The Black Cat* ever again come to the ordeal of the footlights, I can only hope that it may find an audience as sympathetic as that of the Independent Theatre.

THE BLACK CAT

ACT I.

Scene: Denham's Studio. Large highlight window in sloping roof at back. Under it, in back wall, door to landing. l of the door the corner is curtained off for model's dressing-room. r of door a large Spanish leather folding screen, which runs on castors, shuts off from the door the other corner, in which is a "throne," pushed up against the wall. Above the "throne" hangs a large square mirror in a carved black frame. In front of the "throne" is a light couch of Greek form, without back.

Fireplace, with chimney-breasts panelled in old oak, and high overmantel, in which are shelves and cupboards, l.

Against r wall an old oak cabinet, with carved cornice, and inlaid panelled doors. Close beside it stands on a pedestal a bust of Demeter. Near the cabinet, halfway up stage r c, an easel, on which is seen the back of a large picture.

Beyond the fireplace, and at right angles to it, a large sofa, or lounge, with square ends and back, broad low seat, loose cushions, and valance. In front of the fireplace an armchair, with a book face downward on one arm.

The walls of the studio are distempered in greenish-blue, the curtains of the model's dressing-room are in rich yellow plush or brocade, the couch and sofa covered in greenish-yellow stuffs.

Various artistic properties, tapestries, embroideries, etc., hanging up, or thrown carelessly over Chippendale chairs and the screen.

Canvases leaning against the walls, on which hang designs and figure-studies in chalk and charcoal, with landscape-studies in oil and watercolour, nailed up without much attempt at arrangement.

Near the front, just r of the armchair, an oblong carved oak table, with materials for wood-drawing, paint-box, water in a tumbler, etc., is set end on to the footlights.

At the upper end of this table Undine is discovered, as she sits with a slate and arithmetic book before her, her elbows on the table, her head supported on both hands, holding a slate pencil from which a bit of sponge dangles by a string.

UNDINE.

(*pouting*) I hate these old sums! Mother's always making me do sums in the holidays. It isn't fair. Seven times three is—what's father reading? (*Rises, and takes up the book.*) That's French, I know. Father's always reading French. G.Y.P. Gyp? I wonder what it's about. (*Puts the book down, sits, yawns, and takes up the pencil.*) Seven times three is—twenty-one. Put down one and carry two.

Oh, but it's pence and shillings. I can't do pence and shillings! (*Throws down the pencil; it falls off the table.*) Horrid old things! they're always coming wrong. (*She rises lazily, and stoops to pick up the pencil, then looks round her, stretching her arms and yawning.*) I say, what fun to make a libation to Demeter! I will! Let's see. I wish I had mother's Greek dress. I must have one of father's rags. This'll do. (*Drapes herself in a piece of embroidery, runs up stage, jumps on "throne," and poses before the mirror.*) It's awfully jolly dressing up. But I have no wine. Oh, I know—I'll take some of father's painting water—though it's rather black-and-whity. (*Takes up the glass, and approaches the statue.*) Hail, Demeter! I have no wine for you, but here's some water. (*Makes libation.*) I suppose I should pray for something now. Oh, I do wish you'd stop mother persecuting me in the holidays like this! But you can't, you dear old thing. Father says the old gods are dead. I wish they'd come alive again. (*Crosses to table.*)

(*Enter Denham. Undine drops embroidery, kicks it under the table, and sits.*)

DENHAM.

Well, imp, what's up now? (*He comes to the fireplace, and takes a pipe from the rack.*) Rags again! I shall have to lock them up, I see. (*Takes up the embroidery, and throws it over a chair.*) Get to your work at once! Sit up straight. (*He crosses l, seats himself in the arm-chair, lights his pipe, and takes up the book, Undine resumes her crouched position at the table.*)

UNDINE.

(*pouting*) It's very hard to have to do sums in the holidays.

DENHAM.

(*crosses to table behind Undine*) You are behind your class, you know. (*Looking over her.*) Well, seven times three?

UNDINE.

Let's see—twenty-one?

DENHAM.

And how many shillings in that?

UNDINE.

I suppose two shillings and one penny.

DENHAM.

Nonsense! Don't suppose anything so un-English. How many pence in a shilling?

UNDINE.

Twelve—I suppose.

DENHAM.

Well, twelve from twenty-one leaves—
(*Undine counts on her fingers*)
How many?

UNDINE.

About eight, I think.

DENHAM.

Try again, stupid!

UNDINE.

But, father, I think there *ought* to be ten pence in a shilling.

DENHAM.

Why *ought* there, you monkey?

UNDINE.

Oh, because then, don't you see, you could count on your fingers all right, but now there are too many pennies for your fingers, and so you never can tell how many are over.

DENHAM.

Very convenient. But come now, twelve from twenty-one?

UNDINE.

(*counting again*) Nine?

DENHAM.

(*resuming his book*) All right then. Down with it in the pence column, and get on.

UNDINE.

(*kissing him*) Oh, you jolly old father! I should like to do my sums with you always.

DENHAM.

Heaven forbid! Get on! Get on! (*Crosses to chair l.*)

(*A pause.*)

UNDINE.

Father! *Father!*

DENHAM.

H'm!

UNDINE.

I say, Father!

DENHAM.

Do let me read in peace.

UNDINE.

But, father—

DENHAM.

Well?

UNDINE.

Do the Greeks worship Demeter now?

DENHAM.

No, not now.

UNDINE.

The old Greeks were the cleverest people that ever lived, and they had the nicest gods. Don't you wish there were goddesses now, father? (*Rises, and leans against table.*)

DENHAM.

(*absently*) Yes, of course.

UNDINE.

Goddesses sometimes fell in love with *people*, father—didn't they?

DENHAM.

People who didn't happen to be gods? It did occur sometimes, they say.

UNDINE.

And one might fall in love with you, father. That *would* be fun!

DENHAM.

That would be awful. But do stop this chatter, and get on.

UNDINE.

She'd give *me* all sorts of jolly things.
(*A pause.*)
Mrs. Denham (outside the door) In a quarter of an hour will do, Jane.

DENHAM.

Here comes mother!

UNDINE.

Oh, bother these horrid old sums! (*Flops into chair.*)

(*Enter Mrs. Denham, with flowers. She comes to the cabinet to place them in a vase, and sees the water spilt.*)

MRS. DENHAM.

What's all this mess? What have you been doing, miss? (*Crosses to Undine.*)

UNDINE.

(*rising and standing before her*) Please, mother, I only made a libation.

MRS. DENHAM.

You naughty, *wicked* girl! Oh, this wicked, *wicked* waste of time!

UNDINE.

(*whimpering*) But, mother, I only—

MRS. DENHAM.

Hold your tongue, miss. Don't attempt to make excuses. (*Steps back, looks at Undine.*) And just *look* at that pinafore, that was put on you clean this morning, and now it is all over dirt! You have been climbing trees again.

UNDINE.

(*whimpering*) I wasn't climbing trees. I only climbed *one* tree.

DENHAM.

(*aside*) Well parried!

MRS. DENHAM.

Oh, these mean prevarications! If I take my eye off you for a moment, you disobey me. But you *shall* obey me—you shall obey! (*Shakes the child; she screams.*)

DENHAM.

Dear! Dear!

MRS. DENHAM.

How dare you scream at me like that?

UNDINE.

(*crying*) But you're hurting me.

MRS. DENHAM.

Bear it then, bear it *decently*, without screaming like a beast. Have you done your sums?

UNDINE.

Not all.

MRS. DENHAM.

(*looking at sums*) Only one done, and that not right. Oh, this *wicked* waste of time! You are killing me and killing yourself. When you waste your time you are wasting your life. Why *will* you waste your time?

UNDINE.

I don't know.

MRS. DENHAM.

Then you must be taught to know.

DENHAM.

May I say a word? I am chiefly to blame. We were talking about the Greek gods.

MRS. DENHAM.

Oh well, if *you* encourage her in her laziness, I can do nothing. (*Crosses l as she speaks, then turns suddenly.*) Get out of my sight, miss! It is time for you to go out now. Go away, and take off that pinafore. You are a disgrace to your father and to me. (*Gives her a final shake. Undine runs out screaming.*) Oh dear! Oh dear! There! Listen to that precious daughter of yours, filling the house with her yells. (*She presses her hands over her ears.*) Oh, that child will be the death of me! (*Throws herself down upon the couch.*) She ought never to have been born. Her existence is a mistake and a curse.

DENHAM.

(*sighing*) Yes, we are all mistakes from the ideal standpoint.

MRS. DENHAM.

It makes me mad to think that I—I—should have brought such an idiot into the world!

DENHAM.

Yes, you are an over-populated woman, dear. (*Rises up to her.*) The modern woman is very easily over-populated.

MRS. DENHAM.

You can joke about it, of course. To me it is a serious calamity. (*Weeps.*)

DENHAM.

Well, dear, at least we have not repeated our initial mistake. (*Crosses to picture.*)

MRS. DENHAM.

Do you regret it?

DENHAM.

God forbid! I only regret that our relations were not always strictly platonic. That is the highest practical ideal of the age—modern woman being what she is.

MRS. DENHAM.

Yes, I know you despise me in your heart. You are always sneering at me as a modern woman. What do you mean?

DENHAM.

(*crosses to her*) I agree with Michelet: "*La femme est une malade.*"

MRS. DENHAM.

And what is man?

DENHAM.

(*sits in armchair*) Oh, a sick creature too—that's the worst of it. The world spirit is moulting, and we're all sick together.

MRS. DENHAM.

Phrases, phrases, always phrases! When I am most in earnest you put me off with a jest.

DENHAM.

"If I laugh at any mortal thing, 'tis that I may not weep."

MRS. DENHAM.

(*sobbing*) I know I have disappointed you; I know you are not satisfied with me; I have not made you happy.

DENHAM.

(*starting up and pacing*) Happy? Give me life! Give me life! Happiness can take care of itself. But there is no use in crying "Give, give!" like the horse-leech. If we want impossibilities we must achieve them. (*Crosses r.*)

MRS. DENHAM.

You want incompatible things.

DENHAM.

Of course I do. So do you. Your reason and your instincts are at war, just like mine. That is our sickness.

MRS. DENHAM.

How at war?

DENHAM.

Your reason tells you that woman is independent, self-sufficing. Your instincts cry feebly for passion, that savage outlaw which still lies in wait for the modern woman, to carry her whither she would not. Hence your lapse from strict agnostic morality into matrimony, bondage, subjection, and the mistake, Undine.

MRS. DENHAM.

That child has come between us. I think children often do.

DENHAM.

Is that one of the *necessary* horrors of matrimony?

MRS. DENHAM.

Heaven help me, that girl drives me mad!

DENHAM.

Nerves, nerves, as usual. She irritates you, and you irritate her. The mere presence of a child sets your teeth on edge. (*Crosses, and sits r of table.*)

MRS. DENHAM.

My brain has been torn to pieces by children all my life. I was a slave to my own brothers and sisters, because I was the eldest.

DENHAM.

That was very hard, I know; but your own child is different, surely?

MRS. DENHAM.

You seem to think I don't love her?

DENHAM.

Not wisely, but too well—as you love me.

(*Re-enter Undine, dressed to go out, and stands just inside door. Mrs.*

Denham rises, and Undine comes slowly towards her.)

MRS. DENHAM.
Well, dear, have you washed your hands and face?

UNDINE.
Yes, mother.

MRS. DENHAM.
That's my nice clean little girl. (*She embraces and kisses her.*) Why does my little girl make mother angry?

UNDINE.
I don't know.

MRS. DENHAM.
Well, kiss father, and go out while it is fine and bright.

UNDINE.
(*coming behind Denham, and pulling back his head*) Father, I'm going to bring you some buttercups, to put on your table and make your work look pretty.

DENHAM.
Thanks, my wee one. And bring me some sunshine in their cups, like a good little fairy.

UNDINE.
I will.

DENHAM.
(*kissing her*) Good-bye, and now run away.

UNDINE.
I'll bring you some speedwell, mother.

MRS. DENHAM.
(*kissing her*) Thanks, my little Undine.

(*Undine goes out, then peeps back through the door.*)

UNDINE.

And I'll make a daisy chain for Demeter.

MRS. DENHAM.

That *will* be pretty. Good-bye.

UNDINE.

Good-bye. (*Kisses her hand to Denham.*)
(*Exit Undine.*)

DENHAM.

Well, it isn't such a very wicked idiot, after all. Now is it? (*Crosses l, and sits.*)

MRS. DENHAM.

Oh, she is good enough when she hasn't to do what she dislikes. (*Crosses back of table.*)

DENHAM.

Children *are* shockingly human, just like you and me. I wish I could cure you of this intense irritability, Constance.

MRS. DENHAM.

You have often lost your own temper with her when you have tried to teach her anything—often enough. (*Sits l of table.*)

DENHAM.

Yes, it was sheer stupidity. It is a bad educational method. It involves loss of dignity on both sides. Be as stern as you please, but not furious.

MRS. DENHAM.

Furious! (*Rises*) Thank you for the word. (*Crosses r.*) I know I am making myself hated by her and despised by you; but I must do my duty as best I can in the teeth of your cruel criticism. I *must* think of her future.

DENHAM.

(*rises, and lights pipe*) Oh, damn the future—and the past too! You take life too seriously. You are a born self-tormentor, too full of anxiety to live. You have the worst form of the great malady of the age, conscience in the agnostic form. You suffer from the new hysteria.

MRS. DENHAM.

I am not hysterical.

DENHAM.

Pardon me, we are all hysterical nowadays. We have lost our self-possession. You don't kick on the hearthrug and that kind of thing. A bucket of cold water is not "indicated" in your case.

MRS. DENHAM.

It seems to me you are always throwing buckets of cold water over me.

DENHAM.

For heaven's sake, go and reform the world! That is the modern woman's true vocation—and cure. Denounce our sensuality and selfishness from the platform, as well as from the hearth. They are the defects of our qualities. If you don't like us as we are, mould us.

MRS. DENHAM.

(*approaching*) That is what we are trying to do.

DENHAM.

Yes. You have not mastered your material yet. Your technique is a little crude. (*He resumes his seat in the armchair, and puts down his pipe as she comes.*)

MRS. DENHAM.

(*kneeling beside him*) Why will you push me away from you, Arthur? You know I only want to be your wife. You are always implying that our marriage is a failure. Why not say it directly?

DENHAM.

We are creatures of the transition. We have not quite found the new centre of equilibrium. Marriage, except as a symbol, is either a superfluous bond or the consecration of a mistake. You have taught us this great truth, anyhow.

MRS. DENHAM.

Why did you get married then?

DENHAM.

Practically it is still a necessary evil, like war and politics. The brute world, howling, forces us into bonds. It is our business to adjust them so as to gall us as little as possible.

MRS. DENHAM.

(*starting up, crosses r*) If the bonds gall you so much, break them. Don't spend your breath in this puling talk. If you are tired of me, go! As far as I am concerned, I set you free. Find some other woman, if you can, who will be more satisfactory.

DENHAM.

(*rising, and standing with his back to the fire*) But why one other woman? Why not extend my freedom to two?

MRS. DENHAM.

Two or a dozen, what is it to me?

DENHAM.

A dozen, Constance? Do you take me for a Turk? I have often told you every man should be content with three wives. More than this verges upon polygamy. But blessed is he who finds the three in one!

MRS. DENHAM.

Indeed. Have you found that in Gyp?

DENHAM.

No, not directly; though Gyp fills me with thoughts that do often lie too deep for tears. Her cynicism is always illuminating.

MRS. DENHAM.

I wish I could say the same of yours. But why three, and not a dozen?

DENHAM.

There are only three possible women in the world, the Divine Mistress—

MRS. DENHAM.

And the "Divine Matron"—I have heard this sickening cant before.

DENHAM.

Cant? Philosophy! But don't forget the third, The Divine Virgin—Womanhood fashioning itself independently after its own ideal. She has driven us, naked and ashamed, into the desert of disillusion.

MRS. DENHAM.

Truth, truth—let me have truth, though it kill me! Men are cowards; they dare not face the naked facts of life.

DENHAM.

Men are poets. Facts are but the crude stuff of life. Imagination is all.

MRS. DENHAM.

Oh, if you want romance, had you not better go and look for your Divine Mistress? Perhaps you may find some ugly truths in her too.

DENHAM.

(*laughing*) One woman is surely enough for the purposes of disillusion. It is too late to begin sowing one's wild oats. There are no dangerous women about. If there were one healthy women in the world—(*Crosses to picture.*)

MRS. DENHAM.

Well?

DENHAM.

You might have some cause for jealousy.

MRS. DENHAM.

You would quit the wreck?

DENHAM.

If it were really a wreck—perhaps. But why should it be? (*He takes her in his arms, and kisses her.*) For Heaven's sake, cease to wallow in the mud of pessimism! Have faith in yourself and Nature—or at least Human-nature.

MRS. DENHAM.

Oh, if I could, if I could! (*A knock at the door.*)

DENHAM.

Come in.

(*Enter Jane with a telegram, which she hands to Mrs. Denham.*)

JANE.

Please, m'm, a telegram; the boy's waiting!
(*Mrs. Denham tears open the telegram.*)

MRS. DENHAM.

(*pointing to spilt water*) Just wipe up that water, Jane, and push back this table. (*Jane wipes up water, moves table against r, wall, and takes away Undine's slate and book.*)

MRS. DENHAM.

(*reads*) "In town; will call this afternoon."

JANE.

Is there any answer, m'm?

MRS. DENHAM.

No answer. (*Exit Jane.*) Arthur! this is from Blanche Tremaine. She is in town, and comes here to-day. Let me see; it must be more than ten years since we've met—before we were married.

DENHAM.

Blanche Tremaine? Who is she?

MRS. DENHAM.

My old class-fellow at our college in town. She played in our Greek play. She was just seventeen then.

DENHAM.

Younger than you?

MRS. DENHAM.

Two years. Yes; she must be about eight-and-twenty now. You know I told you about her. She married a Mr. Overton.

DENHAM.

Overton? I seem to have heard the name. Didn't she run away from her husband, or something?

MRS. DENHAM.

Yes, poor thing! He led her an awful life.

DENHAM.

Oh, and then she married the co-respondent! I remember.

MRS. DENHAM.

What an interest you take in these scandals!

DENHAM.

Of course, dear. A scandal is a typical case of the great social disease.

MRS. DENHAM.

She promised to be handsome.

DENHAM.

I wonder whether this woman is a weak fool, or a bold experimenter in the art of life?

MRS. DENHAM.

How so?

DENHAM.

Why, having had the courage to come down from the cross, should she go back to it again?

MRS. DENHAM.

What cross?

DENHAM.

What is woman's cross from the foundation of the world but man, man? The cords are the bonds of marriage, her children are the nails, and love her crown of thorns.

MRS. DENHAM.

Very poetical, no doubt.

DENHAM.

Bitter truth, as you are never tired of demonstrating to me. Do you think the unfortunate cross has not had his share of the torment?

MRS. DENHAM.

Too light a share for his tyranny, cruelty, and, above all, his *mean* hypocrisy. May he burn in some spiritual fire for that!

DENHAM.

So he does; it runs in his veins. Well, something better may come of it, some day. By-the-bye, I expect some men to see my picture.

MRS. DENHAM.

Brynhild?

DENHAM.

Yes, such as she is. (*Crosses* R, *and looks at the picture.*) Another failure, of course. (*Sighs.*)

MRS. DENHAM.

Why will you always speak of your work so despondently?

DENHAM.

Because I want to do better. Vanity, I suppose. (*He comes back towards the fireplace.*)

MRS. DENHAM.

Just move out this sofa. (*They move sofa to* C.) Who are coming?

DENHAM.

Oh, Fitzgerald, of course, and possibly Cyril Vane.

MRS. DENHAM.

That little creature? You know I detest him.

DENHAM.

Why *little*? Do you estimate men of genius by the pound?

MRS. DENHAM.

Men of genius, indeed? The man has a second-hand intellect.

DENHAM.

Really, you sometimes say a good thing—that is, an ill-natured one. How you hate culture!

(*Enter Jane, showing in Fitzgerald.*)

JANE.

Mr. Fitzgerald!

(*Exit Jane.*)

(*Fitzgerald saunters up to Mrs. Denham, stops suddenly, straddling his legs, and shakes hands loosely and absently.*)

FITZGERALD.

Lovely day, eh? Have you heard the news?

DENHAM.

We never have heard the news.

MRS. DENHAM.

You are the only gossip who comes our way.

FITZGERALD.

(*good-humouredly*) Gossip, eh? Oh, you needn't think I mind being denounced from your domestic altar, Mrs. Denham! I know you're dying to hear the last bit of scandal.

MRS. DENHAM.

Take pity on me then.

FITZGERALD.

I know this'll interest you awfully. Pottleton Smith's wife's run away at last. Now wasn't I right? (*Looks smilingly at both for sympathy.*) I always said she would, you know.

MRS. DENHAM.

Poor silly little flirt! I'm very sorry.

FITZGERALD.

(*rubbing his hands*) I'm—I'm awfully glad. It'll be the saving of poor Smith. Though he's awfully cut up about it, of course.

DENHAM.

Did she run away with—any one in particular?

FITZGERALD.

A Captain Crosby or Cosby, or something. He's in some horse regiment, the cavalry or something. He's—he's an awful scamp, a blackleg and all that, but an awfully nice fellow. I met him at Smith's the other day, and they—they—they were carrying on all the time under poor little Smith's nose. (*He saunters absently to the easel and looks at the picture.*) The picture—eh? It's—it's awfully good, you know—an advance on your last.
(*During this speech Denham also goes to the easel.*)

MRS. DENHAM.

Don't you think so?

FITZGERALD.

Yes, it's an advance, decidedly. What is it, eh? I forget.

DENHAM.

Brynhild.

FITZGERALD.

Oh, Brynhild! The horse is awfully good, you know—savage and that; but the woman isn't ugly enough—at least, you haven't quite got the right kind of ugliness, eh?

DENHAM.

Unfortunately I meant her to be beautiful.

MRS. DENHAM.

(*smiling*) And I gave him some sittings, Mr. Fitzgerald.

FITZGERALD.

(*with a genial laugh*) Did you, now? Well, he tried to improve on you—that was it. (*With great conviction to Denham.*) But—but surely you're wrong in that. Brynhild was an ugly, passionate woman. The passionate woman is always ugly. The passionate woman has character, and character is always ugly.

DENHAM.

Yes, I know what you mean. But I thought—no, the thing's a failure. Don't bother about it, but come and sit down. Have a cigarette?

(*Gives him a cigarette.*)

FITZGERALD.

Thanks.
(*They sit down, Fitzgerald lights cigarette, and puffs solemnly before he speaks again.*)
Mrs. Smith (*puff*), you didn't know her well? Did you, Mrs. Denham? (*Puff.*)

MRS. DENHAM.

No—not well.

FITZGERALD.

You know I painted her portrait (*looks at lighted end of cigarette*), portrait (*leans back in his chair, replaces cigarette in his mouth, and puffs again. Then putting his hands behind his head, he stretches out his legs, and looks at the ceiling*), so I knew her like my own sister. (*Puff.*) She was a pretty little devil (*puff*), awfully aristocratic, mind you, vulgar, of course, an'—an' poor refined little Smith just *didn't* drop his H's. (*Puffs, chuckles to himself.*) Yes, she was a born jade. (*Puff.*) I—I liked her awfully. (*Puff.*)

MRS. DENHAM.

You seem to like every one awfully.

FITZGERALD.

(*with fervour, sitting up in his chair, and flinging away his half-smoked cigarette*) So I do. I enjoy the Human Comedy. Now you don't enjoy the Human Comedy a bit.

MRS. DENHAM.

It comes too near me.

DENHAM.

A cab at the door; this may be Vane.

(*Crosses* l *to fire.*)

FITZGERALD.

Vane? That's splendid! He cuts me dead now, because I reviewed his last Society Verses, with some other men's, under the head, "Our Minor Poets," in *Free Lances*.

DENHAM.

Oh, an editorial? Serves you right, you Jack-of-all-trades. How if some brother Minor Critic were to class you as a Minor Painter?

FITZGERALD.

For Heaven's sake introduce me to him.

(*Enter Jane, showing in Vane.*)

JANE.

Mr. Vane!
(*Exit Jane.*)
(*Vane shakes hands languidly with Mrs. Denham and Denham, and stares at Fitzgerald, who smiles genially.*)

DENHAM.

Ah, Vane, glad to see you.

VANE.

How d'ye do? Ah, Mrs. Denham, that tea-gown is charming.

MRS. DENHAM.

Flattery from you, Mr. Vane, is more than flattery. Pray excuse me for a moment.
(*Exit Mrs. Denham.*)

DENHAM.

Fitzgerald, you know Vane, of course?

FITZGERALD.

Upon my word I scarcely know. *Do* we know each other, Vane?

VANE.

My dear Fitzgerald, when will you learn that you can never know me?

(*Crosses to picture.*)

FITZGERALD.

Then, my dear Vane, I must learn to be resigned. (*Fitzgerald turns away, and takes up Gyp. Vane looks at the picture.*) What's this? "Autour du Marriage," eh?

(*Opens book, and reads, then lies on sofa, still reading.*)

VANE.

Ah, the Brynhild! My dear Denham, why *will* you do such things?

DENHAM.

What have I done?

VANE.

Not what you have tried to do—to paint an epic picture.

DENHAM.

Is that wrong?

VANE.

Worse than wrong; it is a *bêtise*. (*Comes to fire, and stands with his back to it.*) You might as well try to write a long poem. Such things are certainly *long*, and as certainly not *poems*. That huge thing is not a picture.

DENHAM.

Ah, you write quatrains. Should no poem exceed four lines?

VANE.

Not only should not, but in our present state of development, *cannot*. The quatrain is the analogue of the Greek gem, the *consummate* flower of the national art of the period. It will take at *least* a century to perfect and exhaust it. Have you seen my book, "Three Quatrains"?

DENHAM.
No; have you published it lately?

VANE.
My dear Denham! I never *publish* anything. In a wilderness of mediocrity obscurity is fame.

DENHAM.
Yes, a well-advertised obscurity. But surely you *have* published poems?

VANE.
Where have you lived, my dear fellow? I breathe a poem into the air, and the world hears. If some one prints it, can I help it? One does not print, wake, and become famous; one becomes famous, and the world awakes, cackles, and prints one.

FITZGERALD.
By-the-bye, Vane, there's a quatrain in your "In the House of Hathor" I wanted to ask you about.

VANE.
Which?

FITZGERALD.
Let me see—it begins:

"I saw a serpent in my Lady's heart"—

VANE.
Ah! spare me the torment of hearing—

FITZGERALD.
Your own lines?

VANE.
Mur-dered!

"I saw the serpent of my Lady's heart,
Lovely and leprous; and a violet sigh
Shook the wan, yellowing leaves of threnody,
Bruised in the holy chalice of my Art."

FITZGERALD.

Ah yes! I didn't quite catch the meaning.

VANE.

Meaning? It is a piece of *mu*-sic, in which I have skilfully e-*lu*-ded all *meaning*.

FITZGERALD.

Oh, I see! (*Resumes his book.*)

DENHAM.

(*to Vane*) Have a cigarette?

(*Denham offers him a cigarette; he takes one absently, then lets it drop back into the box.*)

VANE.

Thanks, no—I never smoke. It has become so vulgar.

DENHAM.

Really? What do you do then—*absinthe*?

VANE.

For the purposes of art it is antiquated. (*He sighs.*) I have tried *haschish*.

DENHAM.

Well?

VANE.

Without distinct results—for one's style, that is.

DENHAM.

Oh!

VANE.

One sometimes sees oneself inventing the Narghilé. It involves the black slave, of course, and might lead to a true retrogressive progress—even to the *Harîm*. One pities the superfluous woman, there are so many about.

DENHAM.

Yet Mormonism seems to be a failure.

VANE.

It was so *dreadfully* upholstered!

DENHAM.

The *Harîm* would be a new field for the collector. How prices would run up!

VANE.

Ah, Denham, never touch a dream with the vulgarity of real things!

(*Crosses to picture.*)

(*Fitzgerald, who has been reading Gyp, suddenly comes forward with the book in his hand, and breaks in.*)

FITZGERALD.

This Gyp's *awfully* good. Who is he, eh?

VANE.

(*with patient scorn*) A woman!

FITZGERALD.

(*with conviction*) To be sure! That makes it—splendid!

(*Chuckles to himself, sits again on sofa, and goes on reading.*)

VANE.

(*looking at picture*) Will you never learn to be an *artist*, Denham? The modern picture should be a painted quatrain, with colours for words—words which say nothing, because everything has been said, but which *suggest* all that has been felt and dreamed. Art is the initiation into a mood, a mystery—a sphinx whose riddle every one can answer, yet no one understand.

FITZGERALD.

(*shutting the book on his finger*) Bravo, Vane! 'Pon my word, I begin to believe in you.

VANE.

I can endure even that.

DENHAM.

I am on the wrong tack then?

VANE.

My dear fellow, look at that canvas. What a method! You are like an amateur pianist who tries laboriously to obtain tone, without having mastered the keyboard. One cannot *blunder* into great art. Only Englishmen make the attempt. You are a nation of amateurs.

(*He turns away, and sees a sketch on the l wall*) Did you do this?

DENHAM.

My brush did it somehow.

VANE.

Ah! this is exquisite—or would be if you could paint. Why, *why* not learn the technique of your art, and make these notes of a mood, a moment, so as to give real delight?

DENHAM.

Upon my word, Vane, you are right. That sketch is worth a wilderness of Brynhilds. But look here! (*Crosses to picture. He opens a pocket knife, and makes a long cut across the figure of Brynhild.*) There goes a year's work.

FITZGERALD.

(*rising*) By Jove!

VANE.

My dear fellow, I congratulate you. The year's work is not thrown away—now.

(*Re-enter Mrs. Denham.*)

MRS. DENHAM.
Oh, Mr. Vane, what have you made him do?

VANE.
My dear Mrs. Denham, I have saved your husband's reputation for a few months at least. He cannot do anything so *consummately* bad in *less*. Pray, pray, do not try to understand art! Women never can; they have not yet developed the sixth sense—the sense of *Beauty*. But I must really tear myself away.
(*Mrs. Denham sits gloomily on throne, ignoring Vane.*)

DENHAM.
Won't you stay and have some tea?

VANE.
Thanks, no. Lady Mayfair made me promise to go and hear her new tenor. One knows what one has to expect, but one goes.

(*Enter Jane, showing in Miss Macfarlane.*)

JANE.
Miss Macfarlane!
(*Miss Macfarlane shakes hands with Mrs. Denham and Denham, and nods to Fitzgerald and Vane.*)

MISS MACFARLANE.
How d'ye do, Fitz? Ah, Vane! you here? Don't run away.

VANE.
Unfortunately I must. The wounds of our last encounter are not yet healed.

MISS MACFARLANE.
Pshaw, man! *I* don't use poisoned weapons.

VANE.
Ah, Miss Macfarlane, the broadsword is very effective in your hands! (*Going.*)

FITZGERALD.

Oh, Vane, will you dine with me at the Bohemians on Friday? I want you to hear—

VANE.

The Bohemians? Impossible!

FITZGERALD.

You'll see life, at any rate.

VANE.

My dear fellow, I *have* seen life. *Don't* ask me to see it again. It is a painful spectacle. Adieu!
(*Exit.*)

MISS MACFARLANE.

(*looking at picture*) Why, what's all this?

MRS. DENHAM.

Arthur, I shall never forgive you for destroying your picture—just because that wretched little creature was spiteful about it.

DENHAM.

Pooh! He wasn't spiteful. He only told me the truth about it, in his own jargon. I knew it already.

MISS MACFARLANE.

Oh, but it's none so bad, my dear boy—if it's a failure, it's a good wholesome failure. (*Crosses l to fire.*)

(*Enter Jane, showing in Mrs. Tremaine.*)

JANE.

Mrs. Tremaine! (*Exit Jane.*)

MRS. DENHAM.

My dear Blanche!

MRS. TREMAINE.

My dear Constance! (*They embrace.*)

MRS. DENHAM.

My husband, Mrs. Tremaine. Miss Macfarlane, Mr. Fitzgerald. (*She introduces them.*)

FITZGERALD.

(*thrusting the book into his side pocket*) Well, I must run away. (*Crosses* c.)

DENHAM.

Must you go?

FITZGERALD.

Yes—I've—I've a lot of things to do. Good-bye. (*Shakes hands absently.*)

DENHAM.

Oh, Fitz, I want to show you something. Will you excuse me for a moment, Mrs. Tremaine?
(*Exeunt Denham and Fitzgerald.*)

MRS. DENHAM.

Do sit down, and let us have a little quiet talk.
(*They sit down. Mrs. Denham crosses and sits on sofa* r; *Mrs. Tremaine on sofa* l, *and Miss Macfarlane in armchair by fire, quietly observe each other.*)
You are looking splendidly, Blanche.

MRS. TREMAINE.

Yes, I'm in very good form. But you're not looking well—rather pale, you know.

MRS. DENHAM.

I'm a little tired, that's all. I am so glad to see you again. Why have you quite given me up?

MRS. TREMAINE.

Well, you see, I have been rather making a mess of my life, and I have not been much in town. Besides, I was a little shy about coming, after—all my escapades.

MRS. DENHAM.

You know I'm not a censorious person, Blanche. I don't think our conventional morality very admirable, and I never adored the patient Griselda.

MRS. TREMAINE.

You don't know how I feel your kindness, Constance. I have had a hard time of it, so far; but now I have taken my life into my own hands, and I mean to live it out.

MRS. DENHAM.

But your husband? You married again, did you not?

MRS. TREMAINE.

Yes. Fancy a woman making that mistake twice! But, you see, I was in an equivocal position. I had left my first husband, Miss Macfarlane; I don't want to conceal my misdeeds.

MISS MACFARLANE.

Oh, don't expect paving stones from an old woman like me! I judge every case on its own merits. I know what men are, though I've been content to gain my experience at my friends' expense. I tell ye I know more about the ins and outs of marriages than most married women, just as the curler on the bank sees most of the game. You mayn't have been anything worse than a fool, and ye mayn't have been even that.

MRS. TREMAINE.

Thank you. I was a fool, of course. You see, my first marriage was a mistake altogether. It was my mother's doing. I knew nothing of marriage, or love either, for that matter. That came afterwards, and—all the scandal.

MISS MACFARLANE.

And may I ask, young woman, have you run away from your second husband? You say that marriage was a mistake too

MRS. TREMAINE.

No; he is dead now.

MISS MACFARLANE.

But you don't—(*Looks at her dress.*)

MRS. TREMAINE.

No, I don't *afficher* eternal bereavement. We were separated for two years.

MRS. DENHAM.

Poor Blanche! Then it was not a success?

MRS. TREMAINE.

No; it was not a success.

MISS MACFARLANE.

Well, we mustn't ask why?

MRS. TREMAINE.

Oh, I'm in the humour for confession. I think you can understand. We got on well enough while I was—free. But he did the chivalrous thing—asked me to marry him; and I was glad enough to scramble back to the platform of respectability.

MISS MACFARLANE.

Well, I understand that, anyhow.

MRS. TREMAINE.

That seemed to kill the romance, such as it was. I need not go into the sordid details, but we quarrelled finally about money—my money. My husband took to gambling in stocks. But I have managed to keep my little pittance, fortunately. Well, that is enough of my affairs. Have you any children, Constance?

MRS. DENHAM.

One little girl, just nine. Have you any?

MRS. TREMAINE.

No—none.

MISS MACFARLANE.

A woman who has had such unpleasant experiences ought to hate and despise men. But of course *you* don't?

MRS. TREMAINE.

(*laughing*) No—I don't think I hate men exactly. I despise some men heartily.

MISS MACFARLANE.

They're gey ill to live wi', eh?

MRS. TREMAINE.

I don't think marriage suits me, somehow. I suppose it suits some people. But I think it often tends to reduce them to a dead level of commonplace. The artificial bond makes people too sure of each other. It does not do to take love too much for granted, I think. (*Re-enter Denham.*)

MRS. DENHAM.

Well, Arthur, have you got rid of Mr. Fitzgerald?

DENHAM.

Yes—I'm so glad to have made your acquaintance, Mrs. Tremaine.

MRS. TREMAINE.

Thanks. It is so pleasant meeting unconventional people.

MISS MACFARLANE.

(*Rising*) Eh! we've all been getting solemn and lugubrious. I must be going, my dear. Won't you show me your drawing-room? (*Mrs. Denham rises.*) You wanted my advice about curtains, didn't you?

MRS. DENHAM.

Will you excuse me, Blanche? We are refurnishing our drawing-room. I don't want *you* to come just yet. Arthur will entertain you.

DENHAM.

Oh, with pleasure! (*Exeunt Mrs. Denham and Miss Macfarlane.*) How do you think Constance is looking, Mrs. Tremaine? (*Draws chair over, and sits near her.*)

MRS. TREMAINE.

It struck me she was looking rather worn and ill.

DENHAM.

I'm afraid she is.

MRS. TREMAINE.

She has let herself run down too much. Does she go in for exercise—tennis or anything?

DENHAM.

Nothing of the kind, I am sorry to say.
Mrs. Tremaine.
Oh, I could not live without exercise! I used to ride while I could afford it, and I always try to do gymnastics or something.

DENHAM.

I'm sure you're right. Do you intend to stay in town now?

MRS. TREMAINE.

Yes, I hope to get some work. I have enough income to keep me going; but I want some real employment.

DENHAM.

Quite right. (*Rises, and puts log of wood on fire, then stands with tongs in his hand and looks at her; puts down tongs.*) Well, until you get something that suits you, I wish you would give me some sittings. I'll give you the regular model's wages—a shilling an hour—no, I'll give you two—two shillings an hour—there!

MRS. TREMAINE.

Thank you, it is a generous offer. I have sat before without the shillings, and will again with pleasure—if you will promise to talk to me?

DENHAM.

I won't promise, but I shall talk all the same. So you have sat before?

MRS. TREMAINE.

Yes, artists seem to like painting me; I don't know why. I don't profess to be a beauty.

DENHAM.

Of course no woman is beautiful; but some women have the art of persuading you that they are. You have this art.

MRS. TREMAINE.

(*laughing*) Really you are very polite. Am I to take that as a compliment?

DENHAM.

No, as sincere praise. I am never polite to people I like, and I like you.

MRS. TREMAINE.

Thanks. I like to be liked; and I can forgive your want of politeness, if you are never more brutally rude than you have been. I suppose I am to take it as the rudeness of a man of genius?

DENHAM.

No—like all unsuccessful people who worry themselves over art—I am only a man of *some* genius—a very different thing, I assure you.

MRS. TREMAINE.

Are *you* unsuccessful?

DENHAM.

A man who paints pictures that please only his wife is surely unsuccessful? But I don't want to bore you with myself. It only means that I feel we are friends already.

MRS. TREMAINE.

You don't know how pleasant it is to be with people who don't look upon me as a dreadfully wicked woman.

DENHAM.

No doubt, like all persons of distinction, you belong to the criminal classes; but we are all emancipated here.
(*Re-enter Mrs. Denham and Miss Macfarlane, who goes straight to the fire as she speaks.*)

MRS. DENHAM.

Oh, Arthur, that precious black cat of yours!

MISS MACFARLANE.

We've settled the curtains, now for the cat.

DENHAM.

What has he been doing now?

MRS. DENHAM.

In the larder again. Really that beast must be got rid of. I will not stand such abominations any longer.

DENHAM.

Well, don't ask me to be executioner, that's all.

MRS. TREMAINE.

But surely you're not going to kill a black cat? It is awfully unlucky.

(*Miss Macfarlane keeps Mrs. Tremaine under observation.*)

DENHAM.

Are you superstitious?

MRS. TREMAINE.

I suppose I am. Those peacock feathers made me shiver when I came in.

MRS. DENHAM.

Are peacock's feathers unlucky?

MRS. TREMAINE.

Yes; didn't you know that?

MRS. DENHAM.

No.

DENHAM.

Constance is not superstitious. It is her worst fault. A little superstition gives colour to life.

MRS. TREMAINE.

Do let *me* take the cat, Constance!

MRS. DENHAM.

I am sure you are welcome to the beast.

DENHAM.

Thanks, Mrs. Tremaine.

MRS. DENHAM.

Arthur, take Mrs. Tremaine down to have some tea.

DENHAM.

Will you come, Mrs. Tremaine?
(*Exeunt Denham and Mrs. Tremaine.*)

MISS MACFARLANE.

(*retaining Mrs. Denham*) My dear, beware of that woman! (*Crosses to Mrs. Denham.*)

MRS. DENHAM.

Of Blanche—why?

MISS MACFARLANE.

Ye have a husband, that's all.

MRS. DENHAM.

But you don't suppose—

MISS MACFARLANE.

Eh, I suppose nothing. But that woman loves men. I can see it with half an eye.

MRS. DENHAM.

If my husband does not love me, let him leave me. (*Crosses c.*)

MISS MACFARLANE.

Fiddlesticks, my dear; don't go in for heroics. Of course he loves you. Does it follow he can't love another woman into the bargain? They think they can, at any rate.

MRS. DENHAM.

I don't care for such love.

MISS MACFARLANE.

Of course not. But in this world we must make sure of what we can grab; and then we can grab a bit more, and a bit more, maybe.

MRS. DENHAM.

I can trust my husband.

MISS MACFARLANE.

(*coming to Mrs. Denham*) Right; but don't trust him into temptation. Mind you, she's charming. Men haven't been flogged into constancy, as we have. Remember that. I'm not old-maidish, my dear, though I've escaped holy matrimony. I don't profess hatred of men, they're none so much worse than we are; but they're different, and—pardon my strong language—they're damnably brought up. (*They go up stage towards door.*) Beware of that woman, I tell ye. Don't let her get a footing here. And now, give me some tea.

ACT DROP.

ACT II.

Scene: The Studio. Denham discovered at easel near the front r, a small table with colours, etc., beside him, painting Mrs. Tremaine, in a black evening dress. She sits in a chair upon the "throne" a piece of tapestry behind her, up the stage l. Oak table against l wall, above fireplace.

DENHAM.

Head a little more up. No, I don't want you like that.

MRS. TREMAINE.

Come and pose me then.

DENHAM.

All right. (*He poses her, then goes back to the easel.*) By Jove! this is getting serious. This is the best thing I have done.

MRS. TREMAINE.

So you say of them all. This is the third attempt. How many more do you intend to make?

DENHAM.

Oh, I don't know! I should like to go on as long as I could make headway. (*He paints in silence for some time.*) There, I am getting something I never got before—the real woman at last.

MRS. TREMAINE.

May I see?

DENHAM.

For Heaven's sake, don't stir! (*Paints again.*) Blanche!

MRS. TREMAINE.

Well?

DENHAM.

Do you know I was a fool, to say you were not beautiful?

MRS. TREMAINE.

You only spoke the truth.

DENHAM.

It is a higher truth to say you are; and you seem to have grown *more* beautiful this last month.

MRS. TREMAINE.

Oh, I am happier now!

DENHAM.

Happier?

MRS. TREMAINE.

Yes. You don't know what an oasis this studio has been to me. I shall be sorry to go back to the desert.

DENHAM.

Well, I never had a better model. I have learnt a lot since I began to paint you.

MRS. TREMAINE.

I am so glad if I have been of any use. Have you ever painted Constance?

DENHAM.

I have tried; but she's a fidgety sitter, and always looks like an incarnation of despair. (*He approaches her.*) May I arrange these folds a little?

MRS. TREMAINE.

Certainly.

DENHAM.

(*arranging skirt of dress*) That will do. The fan so—head a *little* more to the left—so. (*He goes back, and paints in silence again.*) This is coming splendidly. I dare not do much more to the head.

MRS. TREMAINE.

Can you finish it to-day?

DENHAM.

As much as I can finish anything. (*Paints again in silence.*) I wish Constance had some of your reposeful quality. I can't think what ails her. She gets more irritable and pessimistic every day.

MRS. TREMAINE.
Perhaps you irritate her.

DENHAM.
I? But, good heavens!—(*Stops painting, and looks at her.*)

MRS. TREMAINE.
Yes, I know. You think you are very patient, while you treat her with a—what shall I say?—a sort of contemptuous respect.

DENHAM.
Really? I am sorry if it seems so. I wish I could rouse her out of the slough of despond.

MRS. TREMAINE.
Perhaps she is disappointed?

DENHAM.
We are all disappointed. It is the niggardliness of Nature—the old woman in the shoe. (*Paints again in silence.*) Do you believe in love, Blanche? Still?

MRS. TREMAINE.
(*sighing*) Yes, I think I do. There is not very much else left for one to believe in, nowadays.

DENHAM.
So do I—as a dream.

MRS. TREMAINE.
Ah! You are the pessimist now.

DENHAM.
Why make mad efforts to realise it?

MRS. TREMAINE.
A necessity of our nature, I suppose.

DENHAM.

What does the modern woman desire or expect from a man? You are sick of marriage, it seems.

MRS. TREMAINE.

As it exists—yes.

DENHAM.

Well, the instinctive *amourette* had its poetry—in Arcadia. Keep your hands quiet a moment.

MRS. TREMAINE.

Let me warm them first. Remember we are in the grip of a London May.

DENHAM.

All right—come. (*She comes over to the picture. He stops her.*) No, you must not look yet.

MRS. TREMAINE.

You have become quite a tyrant, do you know?
(*She goes to the fire.*)

DENHAM.

(*taking her hands*) Cold? Yes; I have kept you too long. You have such good hands! I wish I could paint them.

MRS. TREMAINE.

(*kneels at fire, and warms her hands*) One more chance!

DENHAM.

I shall make the most of it. Well, but what do you want? A friendship, passionate and Platonic? Why, it takes all the tyranny of a strong man like Swift to keep instinct within bounds. The victory killed Stella and Vanessa.

MRS. TREMAINE.

Oh, we are more rational now! Then, there were two of them; that was the difficulty there.

DENHAM.

Yes, there were two of them. Except in a desert island, there is always a danger of that.

MRS. TREMAINE.

Why are men so inconstant?

DENHAM.

Why are women so charming—and unsatisfactory? We deceive ourselves, and are deceived, just like you.

MRS. TREMAINE.

You amuse yourselves, and we pay.

DENHAM.

It is the will of God—of Nature, I should say. She is an artist; but as for her morality—

MRS. TREMAINE.

One can't say much for that.

DENHAM.

Art is Nature's final aim. Love is the Art of Arts, and Art is long.

MRS. TREMAINE.

But could you not be a *little* more constant, if you tried?

DENHAM.

Oh, *we* can resist temptation, when we are not tempted—just like women.

MRS. TREMAINE.

Your *capacity* for temptation is wonderful.

DENHAM.

Yes. *We* know our own frailty, *you* never quite realise yours.

MRS. TREMAINE.

What has made you so cynical?

DENHAM.

The bitterness of life. Are your hands warm yet? (*Takes her hands.*)

MRS. TREMAINE.

Yes, I can go back now.
(*She goes back to the "throne." He poses her, and returns to the easel.*)

DENHAM.

(*painting again*) Marriage must certainly be modified. A woman should have some honourable way of escape, when her husband gets tired of her.

MRS. TREMAINE.

(*laughing*) How delicately you put it! But the wife? If you had to bear all you so chivalrously inflict on us in "honourable" marriage, I wonder how many marriages there would be?

DENHAM.

Instinct would be too strong for us still. But we should outscheme Nature. We should invent. What has a woman ever invented since the beginning of the world? Well, you can easily rail us out of marriage. How will you live then?

MRS. TREMAINE.

As we are trying to live now.

DENHAM.

I believe woman's great ambition is to do all the work of the world, and maintain man in idleness.

MRS. TREMAINE.

That would be awful! You would all be artists and minor poets then.

DENHAM.

You, I believe, prefer "the Free Union," as it is called, to marriage?

MRS. TREMAINE.

If it were practicable.

DENHAM.

Ah yes! We can't live innocently and comfortably in "open sin," until the kingdom of heaven comes.

MRS. TREMAINE.

(*laughing*) No, I fear there are still difficulties. But, after all, one can do—well, almost anything; if one does it from conscientious motives—and knows one's way about.

DENHAM.

Yes. And how charming the relationship might be made! Women would really study the art of keeping a lover. But what, in Heaven's name, is the sympathetic modern man to do, who feels that to love one of these creatures of a finer clay, in his rough masculine fashion, is to "insult," or "enslave," or injure her, in one way or another? "I love you, therefore God forbid I should marry you!"—that is the newest gospel.

MRS. TREMAINE.

We are not all such miserable creatures as you imagine. Treat us decently well, and we can stand a good deal, without whining like men—poor persecuted saints!

DENHAM.

It is quite impossible to treat you well in this "imperfect dispensation." Bah! let us talk of something else.

(*Enter Mrs. Denham, dressed to go out.*)

MRS. DENHAM.

This letter has come for you, Blanche, sent on from your house.

MRS. TREMAINE.

Thanks so much. I have been expecting it. Will you excuse me? (*Opens letter and reads.*)

MRS. DENHAM.

I am sorry to interrupt you, Arthur, but I am just going out. Can you give me a cheque?

DENHAM.

Certainly. But first look at this.

MRS. DENHAM.

(*looks at the picture*) Better, I think.

DENHAM.

Eyes too big now?

MRS. DENHAM.

No, not now. Let me have the cheque, and I will go.
(*Denham crosses in front of easel to table, takes cheque book from a
drawer in the table, and writes. Mrs. Tremaine rises and crosses c.*)

DENHAM.

Is that all you have to say?

MRS. DENHAM.

Oh, my opinion is of no value! I think you have improved; but, you
know, I like your ideal work best.

DENHAM.

This is miles ahead of anything I have done.

MRS. DENHAM.

Perhaps—as a piece of painting.

DENHAM.

I am finding my way at last. Here is the cheque.

MRS. DENHAM.

(*crosses l, takes cheque, and crosses c*) You will stay to dinner,
Blanche, of course?

MRS. TREMAINE.

Thanks very much, but I can't possibly.

DENHAM.

I am so sorry, but why?

MRS. TREMAINE.

(*waving the letter, crosses in front of easel, and goes down r*) Work, work! I have got an engagement.

MRS. DENHAM.

I congratulate you.

DENHAM.

But what is it? You have never told us what you have been working at in secret.

MRS. TREMAINE.

No. It might have come to nothing. I am to sing three songs at a private concert.

DENHAM.

A good house?

MRS. TREMAINE.

Capital—and good people to hear me. I may choose my own songs, Italian, German, or English. I have a fortnight to prepare, and I am to be *paid*!

DENHAM.

Brava!

MRS. DENHAM.

You are not going just yet?

MRS. TREMAINE.

No, not immediately. (*Crosses to "throne" and sits again. Denham follows her.*)

MRS. DENHAM.

We shall meet again then. Good-bye!

MRS. TREMAINE.

(*as Denham arranges her skirt*) A bientôt!
(*Exit Mrs. Denham. Denham begins to paint.*)

DENHAM.

Well, you mysterious creature, I think you have chosen your profession well. Your voice is lovely, and your style—well, not bad in these days of execrable singing.

MRS. TREMAINE.

Do you know, it was your praise that made me think seriously of this?

DENHAM.

(*absorbed in painting*) Really? But why would you never sing to me since that evening?

MRS. TREMAINE.

I have been working so hard; I wanted to surprise you.

DENHAM.

And now you will?

MRS. TREMAINE.

Perhaps—some time. (*A pause, Denham painting in silence.*)

DENHAM.

Come down and look at this thing now. I can do no more to it.

MRS. TREMAINE.

(*comes over to the easel, Denham puts down brush and palette*) But this is splendid!

DENHAM.

(*taking pipe*) Better, isn't it? (*Crosses l, to table, and strikes a match.*)

MRS. TREMAINE.

Oh *yes*! But how you *have* flattered me! I shall be reduced to a proper humility when I look in the glass. (*Turns and glances at mirror, then again at picture.*)

DENHAM.

Never mind the glass. That's how I see you.

MRS. TREMAINE.

(*crosses c and drops him a curtsey*) Thank you, sir. An uncynical compliment at last!

DENHAM.

(*bowing*) 'Tis but your due, madam, I protest. Come, sit down, and let us be lazy. (*Pushes armchair round for Mrs. Tremaine, takes chair from "throne" and sits near her.*) We have worked very hard. Do you ever go to the theatre?

MRS. TREMAINE.

Sometimes.

DENHAM.

Does it amuse you?

MRS. TREMAINE.

Oh yes! I like a good three act farce.

DENHAM.

So do I. But our serious plays are amusing in a deeper way—now that we have begun timidly to scratch the surface of things. I wonder, if you and I were put on the stage, what they would say of us?

MRS. TREMAINE.

But there is nothing to make a play about in *us*.

DENHAM.

They would certainly say there was "no situation," though perhaps—

MRS. TREMAINE.

What *is* a situation?

DENHAM.

Oh, you know—something threadbare, the outraged husband driving his erring wife about the stage—all that sort of thing.

MRS. TREMAINE.

I love an outraged husband; they are so magnificently moral!

DENHAM.

Unfortunately I am on no such pinnacle. (*Rises.*) I can only humbly ask you, when will you sit again?

MRS. TREMAINE.

Oh, now that you have painted that masterpiece, I must resign the privilege of being your model.

DENHAM.

That is unkind of you, Blanche. But why? (*Puts his pipe down.*)

MRS. TREMAINE.

You can't go on painting *me* for ever.

DENHAM.

I *shall* go on painting you for ever. But you will surely give me an occasional sitting?

MRS. TREMAINE.

No; I must be stern. (*Rises and crosses c.*) I must work seriously now.

DENHAM.

At least you'll come and see us? You'll come and sing the savageness out of this bear?

MRS. TREMAINE.

No; I must go back into the desert.

DENHAM.

Seriously?

MRS. TREMAINE.

Yes.

DENHAM.

I knew it must come to an end, Blanche. (*Crosses c.*) Well, we have had a good time.

MRS. TREMAINE.

Yes. It has been pleasant here.

DENHAM.

You have been my good genius. Do you know, I was getting sick of it all before you came?

MRS. TREMAINE.

Sick of what?

DENHAM.

Of myself, of art, of life.

MRS. TREMAINE.

That was foolish. I am glad if I have reconciled you to existence.

DENHAM.

You have made me alive again, opened a door to new possibilities, let me out into the sunshine.

MRS. TREMAINE.

Well, don't go back into the shadow. (*Taking her hat, she goes towards mirror.*)

DENHAM.

No. I will go forward.

MRS. TREMAINE.

That is right; and now I must go. (*About to take cloak.*)

DENHAM.

No, you must not go yet. Come and sit upon your throne once more. (*Mrs. Tremaine stops.*)

MRS. TREMAINE.

But you are not going to paint again?

DENHAM.

No. I only want to look at you. Do grant me this last grace! (*He replaces chair on "throne."*)

MRS. TREMAINE.

(*puts down hat, and crosses l*) Really you are too absurd! (*She sits on the "throne."*)

DENHAM.

(*crosses c*) Thanks. And now I want you to read something. (*Goes to table and takes paper from drawer.*)

MRS. TREMAINE.

What must I read?

DENHAM.

This sonnet.

MRS. TREMAINE.

Your own?

DENHAM.

Mine—and yours. Read it aloud.

MRS. TREMAINE.

I did not know you were a poet.

DENHAM.

Every man is a poet once in his life. You have made me one. (*He sits at her feet on the "throne."*)

MRS. TREMAINE.

(*Reads*):

To a Beautiful Woman.

(*Looks down at him and smiles.*)

> *Some women are Love's toys, kiss'd and flung by,*
> *Some his pale martyrs: thou art womanhood,*
> *Superbly symbol'd in rare flesh and blood.*
> *Eternal Beauty, she for whom we sigh,*
> *Dowers thee with her own eternity;*
> *Thou art Love's sibyl: in proud solitude*
> *O'er his old mysteries thy deep eyes brood,*
> *And at thy feet his rich dominions lie.*
> *Hast thou a heart? Let me desire it still.*
> *Torture my heart to life with thy disdain;*
> *Yet smile, give me immortal dreams, still be*

My Muse, my inspiration, vision, will!
I ask no pity, I demand but pain:
And if I love thee, what is that to thee?

It sounds very well; but I'm afraid I don't quite understand it.

DENHAM.

That is the highest praise you could give it; if it be unintelligible it *must* be fine. It means *"mes hommages!"* (*Kisses her hand.*) And now come down! (*He hands her down from the "throne".*)

MRS. TREMAINE.

(*with a shy laugh, crosses* r) But you don't mean to say that you have said all those fine words about me?

DENHAM.

Yes—*to* you, Blanche. I love you. What is that to you? (*Comes down to fire.*)

MRS. TREMAINE.

It is very flattering, no doubt, to be made love to in pretty verses. (*With a mocking smile.*) Is this your "situation" at last?

DENHAM.

Yes, it is a situation.

MRS. TREMAINE.

(*sharply*) Oh, I see! I am to be a sort of lay figure for your poetry, as well as your painting; the Laura of this new Petrarch. Thank you! (*She bows with a little laugh.*)

DENHAM.

I love you, Blanche, I love you!

MRS. TREMAINE.

Say it in verse as much as you like. It does not sound nice in prose. Don't let us make fools of ourselves, Mr. Denham.

DENHAM.

We can't avoid it, Mrs. Tremaine. To do it with dignity is all that can be expected of us.

MRS. TREMAINE.

(*with increased vexation*) That's impossible. (*Crosses* r, *and takes cloak.*) Don't let us spoil a pleasant friendship with nonsense of this kind. Let me keep that—and your sonnet—and good-bye! (*She comes down to* l c. *Denham takes her cloak and puts it on her, keeping his hands on her shoulders.*)

DENHAM.

As you please. Call it friendship, or anything you like. To me it is new life. You have simply taken possession of me from the first—imagination, heart, soul, everything. I live in you, I see your face, I hear your voice, I speak to you when you are absent, just as if you were present. I call you aloud by your name—Blanche, Blanche!

(*She starts away from him, and the cloak remains in his hands.*)

MRS. TREMAINE.

Hush, hush, Mr. Denham! I ought not to listen to such words from you. I never dreamed—

DENHAM.

(*throwing cloak over back of sofa*) I know, I know. Women never do; they go on their way like blindfold fates. Is there such a thing as a magnetic attraction—affinity? I never believed in it till I saw you.

MRS. TREMAINE.

(*laughs nervously*) With how little ingenuity men make love!

DENHAM.

Don't laugh at my raving, you cruel Blanche! I know it sounds as foolish as a schoolboy's valentine; but it is as sincere—and inadequate. Words are stupid things. (*He takes her hands, and looks in her face.*)

MRS. TREMAINE.

Do let us part friends. If you are in earnest, you must know this is wicked as well as foolish.

DENHAM.

Yes, it is always wicked to snatch a moment's supreme happiness in this world. *If* I am in earnest! You know I am in earnest! (*He strokes her hair, then, as she turns away, he puts his arm round her waist and draws her to him.*) Blanche, my beautiful Blanche! I did not mean to say all this, but it was too strong for me.

MRS. TREMAINE.

Let me go, Mr. Denham!

DENHAM.

(*releasing her*) Well, go! (*Crosses l.*) Go, if you can!

MRS. TREMAINE.

(*angrily*) I can and will. (*Turns to take her cloak.*)

DENHAM.

Do you know, Blanche, I thought you loved me?

MRS. TREMAINE.

(*turning sharply*) Then you were more foolish than I thought. (*Softening.*) Perhaps I was to blame, but I meant nothing wrong.

DENHAM.

Oh, I acquit you completely! We drifted—that was all. Jest sometimes turns to earnest. Well, go—go with those tears in your eyes. There is nothing worth crying about—more than is becoming.

MRS. TREMAINE.

Don't say unkind things to me. I can't bear them, though I suppose I deserve them. I liked you, and your admiration flattered my vanity; and I suppose I may have made you think I cared more for you than—I did.

DENHAM.

Well, you don't love me. What does it matter? *I* love *you*; that is the important thing to me. I thank you for that eternal possession. Let it be a dream, austere and pure. Passion has its own ascetic cell, where it can fast and scourge itself. I ask you for nothing, Blanche. I am yours wholly. Do what you like with me.

MRS. TREMAINE.

Go back to your wife.

DENHAM.

Yes—my poor Constance! Well, Blanche, at least you and I can't utterly spoil each other's lives. We can't *marry* each other.

MRS. TREMAINE.

Don't say any more. Let us forget all this.

DENHAM.

Forget? No. But we must renounce. You, too, will wear the sack-cloth.

MRS. TREMAINE.

(*petulantly*) Why should *I* wear sackcloth?

DENHAM.

My dear Blanche, you are not such a fine coquette as you imagine. (*Going close up to her.*) Do you think I can't read those beautiful eyes of yours? You love me! Your love fills the air like the fragrance of a flower. (*He clasps her in his arms.*)

MRS. TREMAINE.

(*impatiently*) Suppose I did. *Après?*

DENHAM.

You do love me, Blanche? (*Kisses her.*)

MRS. TREMAINE.

(*with inward rage*) Yes, I love you. (*Suddenly embracing him.*) I love you! What does it matter?

DENHAM.

Oh, it is the eternal tragedy! We must renounce.
(*Half releasing her.*)

MRS. TREMAINE.

Why must we renounce? Now that you have gone so far, why turn back?

DENHAM.

(*releasing her*) It is the least of evils. How should I hide you from the world's vile slanders? Let us keep our dream unsullied.

(*Crosses* l.)

MRS. TREMAINE.

I have been through the fire already, and could face it again—for a man I loved, and who loved me.

DENHAM.

But it would scorch you worse than before. Then, Constance!

MRS. TREMAINE.

(*with scorn*) Ay, Constance! You ought to have thought of her before. (*Passionately.*) Why have you spoken to me? Why have you compelled *me* to speak, if you are not bold enough to break the bonds that are strangling you?

DENHAM.

Because I must. Don't tempt me, Blanche. We shall sometimes meet, look in each other's eyes, and keep our secret. It is best so. I love you so much that I would save you from yourself.

MRS. TREMAINE.

I don't understand such love. (*Turns away* r.)

DENHAM.

Women never do. They prefer being treated like dogs. Is it nothing that we have met heart to heart for one sweet moment, that you have rested a moment in my arms? To me it is a glimpse of the unattainable heaven of love. (*Going up to her.*) Kiss me once, Blanche, and farewell!

MRS. TREMAINE.

It must be for ever, then.

(*They kiss, and remain clasped in each other's arms.*)

(*Enter Mrs. Denham suddenly.*)

MRS. DENHAM.

Arthur! Oh, I see, I am in the way! (*She is about to retire.*)

DENHAM.

(*coming forward*) No; come in, Constance. Blanche is going away.
(*Crosses* l.)

MRS. DENHAM.

Indeed! I must apologise for interrupting a very pretty parting
scene. Had I not better retire until your interesting *tête-à-tête* is
over?

DENHAM.

There is no necessity. It is over.

MRS. DENHAM.

(*coming down* c) Then may I ask for an explanation of—what I
have unintentionally seen?

DENHAM.

Certainly. You have a right to ask anything you please.

MRS. DENHAM.

Well?

DENHAM.

We have had our fit of madness. Now we are sane, and Blanche is
going away. That is all. (*Goes to table* l.)

MRS. DENHAM.

Oh, indeed! Arthur, Arthur, I trusted in your love, and you have
betrayed me. You love this woman!

MRS. TREMAINE.

(*coming down*) Let *me* speak, Constance. If there be a fault or a
folly in the matter, it is mine. You hate me; you have cause. I
have—been vain and selfish. I thought, like many another woman,
I could play with temptation—

MRS. DENHAM.

(*with fierce scorn*) And with your experience, too!

MRS. TREMAINE.

I know my own weakness now. But I am going away, Constance—going away out of your lives for ever. If I have sinned, I can expiate.

MRS. DENHAM.

Expiate! A fine word, with which we drug our consciences. You have treated me basely, cruelly, treacherously, and you *will expiate*! A common thief can at least make restitution. Can you do that? You are going away, taking my husband's heart with you. Can you give me that back? I would rather you had stabbed me—killed me with one merciful stroke.

MRS. TREMAINE.

No, I am taking nothing with me—nothing but my own folly. I have been the toy of your husband's imagination, that is all. To him this has been nothing more than a passing flirtation.

MRS. DENHAM.

You love him, and he loves you. Don't palter with the truth. (*Crosses* l.)

MRS. TREMAINE.

Yes, I love him; but he does *not* love me. If either of us have cause for jealousy, it is not you.

MRS. DENHAM.

(*laughing bitterly*) You jealous of me? You dare to say this? (*Moves towards door.*)

DENHAM.

For God's sake, Constance, don't let us lose our heads! Let us be just to each other. This was our fate. Call it our fault, if you will. We have been in the grip of a strong temptation; but we have given each other up.
(*Mrs. Tremaine puts on her hat, cloak, and gloves.*)

MRS. DENHAM.

(*coming back* c) Given each other up! Do you think you can satisfy *me* with such phrases? I am to be your faithful wife, I suppose; content with whatever poor shreds of affection you choose to dole out to me, while all your thoughts are with another woman. It would have been more straightforward, (*with withering contempt*) I won't say more *manly*, to have told me plainly: "I cannot love you, therefore I must leave you." But this intrigue behind my back is despicable—despicable!

DENHAM.

(*pacing about angrily*) Intrigue! Yes, of course. You always knew the value of an ugly word. (*Restraining himself.*) Otherwise you have put the abstract morality of the thing admirably. But I am unprincipled enough not to want to desert my wife and child, merely because I love another woman.

MRS. DENHAM.

Oh yes, compromise, compromise, the god that men worship! Go to your mistress, if she will have you. I renounce you.

MRS. TREMAINE.

(*laughing bitterly*) Excuse me, but our little comedy is played out. I am out of the story. (*Exit.*)

DENHAM.

(*crosses up to door*) Stay, Blanche! You must not go like this. One moment, Constance.
(*Exit, following Mrs. Tremaine.*)

MRS. DENHAM.

(*flinging herself down on the sofa*) My God! my God! what am I to do? How am I to live? I cannot stay in this house with a man who no longer loves me. Oh, if *she* had not come between us! Yes, yes! A pretty face and a little flattery outweighs a life's devotion. Oh, it is hard, it is hard!

(*A pause. Then enter Undine.*)

UNDINE.

Mother! Are you sick?

MRS. DENHAM.

No, dear. I have a headache, that's all.

UNDINE.

I'm sorry, mother. (*Kisses her.*)

MRS. DENHAM.

(*clasping her in her arms*) Well, what does my little girl want now?

UNDINE.

May I go and play with Maude and Bertie after school to-morrow, and stay to tea?

MRS. DENHAM.

You may go and play; but you know I cannot let you stay to tea.

UNDINE.

Oh, but why? They want me to stay to tea.

MRS. DENHAM.

You know you broke your promise the last time, and stayed without leave.

UNDINE.

But I forgot—I really did.

MRS. DENHAM.

You must be taught not to forget. Now I'll give you one more chance. You may go and play, but you *must* come back to tea. Promise me that you will.

UNDINE.

Well, I promise. But it's very hard to remember promises, when you want to do a thing very much.

MRS. DENHAM.

Yes; but you must learn to be trustworthy. Now run away. (*Exit Undine.*)
The child hates me, I know. I suppose I must expect nothing but dislike and contempt. She is her father's child. I wish I had died long ago. (*Crosses* r, *and sits by table.*)
(*A pause, then re-enter Denham.*)

DENHAM.

Well, Blanche is gone.

MRS. DENHAM.

(*listlessly*) Indeed!

DENHAM.

(*seating himself*) To the advanced moralist, I know I am an object of contempt. I can't help that.

MRS. DENHAM.

(*rising*) If you have come here to insult me with sneering speeches, I will go. (*Crosses* c *up stage.*)

DENHAM.

Let us leave this tone of falsetto, Constance, and speak seriously to each other. I have come to you for help in this crisis of our lives. Sit down. (*Gives her a chair.*)

MRS. DENHAM.

(*sitting*) To me! That is very magnanimous.

DENHAM.

No. You are the only friend I have.

MRS. DENHAM.

Well?

DENHAM.

You bid me desert the nest?

MRS. DENHAM.

Since it is cold.

DENHAM.

Is it so cold?

MRS. DENHAM.

Need you ask? (*Shivers.*) If you do not quit it, I will.

DENHAM.

I have no doubt you will do what you think right. The question is, what *is* right? (*Rises, and looks at her.*)

MRS. DENHAM.

(*looking away from him*) You have always held yourself aloof from me. All my love has been powerless to gain an entrance into your heart. Now it is too late. I give up the useless struggle.

(*Crosses* l, *and sits in armchair crouching over fire.*)

DENHAM.

(*passionately*) Held myself aloof! Good God! is that my fault? You want something that you can neither excite nor reciprocate. (*With a sudden change of manner.*) No—it was my own dulness of heart. My poor Constance! This has been a revelation for us both. But you don't know how I have tried to conform to your ideals—to spare you in every possible way.

MRS. DENHAM.

(*bitterly*) Yes, you have been very patient, very forbearing, no doubt. It is better to kill a woman than to tolerate her.

DENHAM.

You did not always think so. You wanted love in the form of an unselfish intellectual friendship. Well, I have tried to love you unselfishly, God knows! It is an impossible basis for marriage. However, we *are* married. May we not at least be friends? (*Comes and stands by her chair.*) Do you think marriage exists for the sake of ideal love? What about Undine?

MRS. DENHAM.

I presume you will provide for your daughter?

DENHAM.

Is she not yours too?

MRS. DENHAM.

She loves you; she does not love me. I suppose I don't deserve it. I know you think I have been a bad wife, a bad mother. I am better out of your way. (*Weeps.*)

DENHAM.

This is morbid. Oh, if I could have cured you! Constance! (*He caresses her hair.*)

MRS. DENHAM.

Don't touch me! It is an insult.

DENHAM.

(*sighing*) I suppose I have lost the right of comforting you. (*Crosses* r.)

MRS. DENHAM.

I don't want your pity. (*Rises.*)

DENHAM.

Perhaps I want yours.

MRS. DENHAM.

(*indignantly*) Suppose *you* had caught *me* in a low intrigue, and I had dared to speak to you as you have spoken to me—without so much as a word that implied sorrow or repentance, what would you say to me?

DENHAM.

I would ask your forgiveness humbly enough if that were of any use. It isn't, I know. Sins that are instinctive, not of malice, lie too deep for forgiveness.

MRS. DENHAM.

A fine aphorism, no doubt. How does it apply?

DENHAM.

You can't forgive insults that were not intended, and a "low intrigue" which was only a mad, selfish leap for life. Let us part then, if you please. We missed our moment for passion long ago, if that is what you want.

MRS. DENHAM.

My want aches deeper. Well, you love another woman. Go to her. Let her make you happy if she can.

DENHAM.

Why should I go to her? I love her as a dream; let me keep her as a dream. Why should I spoil her life as I have spoiled yours?

MRS. DENHAM.

You could not spoil her life as you have spoiled mine, if you love her.

DENHAM.

(*half to himself as he comes down stage* r) It is a magnificent temptation. To give one's passion its full reckless swing, to feel the blood bounding in one's veins—

MRS. DENHAM.

Why not? And leave the woman to pay.

DENHAM.

(*with a reckless bitterness*) Yes, that's the devil of it. You have put me out of conceit with love. Your chamber of horrors haunts my imagination. If a woman could give us all she promises, we should be like gods. But she can't. Why should we worry about it? Why ask for cakes and ale, when sermons and soda-water are so much better for us?

MRS. DENHAM.

You never loved me. Your cakes and ale are no concern of mine. (*Crosses to table. Knock at door.*) Come in!

(*Enter Jane, showing in Miss Macfarlane.*)

JANE.

Miss Macfarlane!
(*Exit.*)

MISS MACFARLANE.

Well, my dear, how are you all? Eh! but what's the matter now? (*She looks from one to the other.*) Mrs. Tremaine, I suppose?

DENHAM.

Mrs. Tremaine has gone away—back to the desert, as she says.

MISS MACFARLANE.

And high time for her, too. Upon my word, I should like to give that fascinating person a bit of my mind.

DENHAM.

And me too, I am sure.

MISS MACFARLANE.

Well, as you ask me, Mr. Denham, I think your conduct in bringing that woman into the house, and carrying on a flirtation with her under your wife's eyes, was simply abominable. It was an insult to Constance. Did ye ever consider that? It was not the conduct of a gentleman!

DENHAM.

No, a gentleman should throw a decent veil of secrecy over his—flirtations. But, you see, if I had done that, I should have been a hypocrite; now I'm only a brute.

MISS MACFARLANE.

Oh, my dear boy, don't be a brute, and then you needn't be a hypocrite. There's the way out of that.

DENHAM.

It is a narrow way.

MISS MACFARLANE.

If ye can't have good morals, at least have good manners. (*Crosses l.*)

DENHAM.

Oh, good manners are becoming obsolete. They are too much trouble for this Bohemian age. Ladies and gentlemen went out with gold snuffboxes and hooped petticoats; we are trying to be men and women now, frankly and brutally.

MISS MACFARLANE.

Eh! and I suppose ye thought ye were learning to be a man by playing at Adam and Eve with Mrs. Tremaine?

DENHAM.

(*crosses r*) We drifted, we drifted.

MISS MACFARLANE.

A man has no *right* to *drift*, Mr. Denham. Ye have to look before ye, and pick your steps in this world; at any rate, when other people are hurt by your slips. An irresponsible animal isn't a man.

DENHAM.

I wish we had a Court of Love, Miss Macfarlane, with you for President. But, if you'll excuse me, I shall leave you with Constance now. I know she would like to speak to you. (*Exit.*)

MISS MACFARLANE.

Well, my dear, what is it? You see I claim the privilege of an old friend.

MRS. DENHAM.

I can bear my burden alone, Miss Macfarlane. (*Crosses* c.)

MISS MACFARLANE.

Of course you can, my dear. But there's no harm in a little honest sympathy.

MRS. DENHAM.

(*sobbing and embracing her*) Oh, I beg your pardon! But I am so miserable, so miserable!

MISS MACFARLANE.

There, there—that's right. (*Leads Mrs. Denham to sofa.*) And now you can tell me or not, just as you like.

MRS. DENHAM.

What is there to tell? It is all over—that is all. (*She sits down, weeping.*)

MISS MACFARLANE.

But what's all over? We sometimes think things are all over, when they're only beginning. A thunderstorm's not the Day of Judgment. It clears the air.

MRS. DENHAM.

This *is* the Day of Judgment for me. I am weighed in the balance and found wanting. I wish I were dead.

MISS MACFARLANE.

Nonsense, dear; you're no failure. But I'll tell ye what the two of you are—a pair of fools; that's what you are. You should have put your foot down, my dear. *She* was the Black Cat you ought to have got rid of, and nipped this business in the bud. I don't know how far it has gone. Does he want to run away with her?

MRS. DENHAM.

No; he professes to have given her up.

MISS MACFARLANE.

Then he's none such a fool, after all. That woman would have led him a pretty dance!

MRS. DENHAM.

He loves her—let him go to her. (*Rises and crosses* l. *Stopped by Miss Macfarlane.*)

MISS MACFARLANE.

Fiddlesticks, my dear! Don't force him into her arms. Mind you, he has vowed to cherish you as well as to love you; and how can he do that if you drive him away? Do ye remember one of his misquotations from Byron:

> *"Man's love is from his life a thing apart,*
> *'Tis woman's main subsistence?"*

There's truth in that.

MRS. DENHAM.

Men make love, like everything else, a mere *game*.

MISS MACFARLANE.

Ay, you're right there. But until *we* hold the purse strings, it's hard to keep them to the strict rules o' the game.

MRS. DENHAM.

That is a vile injustice! I may not be able to fight on equal terms, but I will never submit. If he does not go, I will. (*Crosses* r.)

MISS MACFARLANE.

Don't wreck your lives for a man's passing fancy. If that's your new morality, I prefer the old. Don't turn this comedy into a tragedy. That's all very well on the stage, but we're not acting an Ibsen play; it doesn't pay in real life.

MRS. DENHAM.

A good tragedy is better than a bad comedy.

MISS MACFARLANE.

Come to your room, my dear. Have your cry out, sponge your eyes, and we'll have a quiet talk.

MRS. DENHAM.

Oh, this sense of failure! It will drive me mad!

ACT DROP.

ACT III.

Scene: The Studio. Mrs. Denham lying on sofa r c, *a shawl over her feet, her face buried in her hands, moaning inarticulately. Table as in* Act II.

(*Enter Denham excitedly.*)

DENHAM.

Constance!

MRS. DENHAM.

(*moving and raising her head*) Well?

DENHAM.

Where is Undine?

MRS. DENHAM.

Undine?

DENHAM.

Yes. Do you know where she is?

MRS. DENHAM.

In her room, I suppose. I told her to stay there.

DENHAM.

She is not in the room—not in the house.

MRS. DENHAM.

But—I locked the door.

DENHAM.

She must have got out of the window.

MRS. DENHAM.

She can't have dropped from the balcony.

DENHAM.

Stay a moment. (*Exit.*)

MRS. DENHAM.

(*resuming her position*) No peace! No peace!
(*Re-enter Denham.*)

DENHAM.

Yes. Her skipping rope is tied to the rails. She must have dropped into the garden. She's as active as a cat.

MRS. DENHAM.

And as sly. Another act of disobedience.

DENHAM.

Tell me, Constance, have you had a—I mean, have you punished her?

MRS. DENHAM.

(*bitterly*) I beat her, since you are kind enough to inquire—beat her for her utter untrustworthiness and mean prevarication. I said I would, if she disobeyed me again.

DENHAM.

Poor little wretch! But what did you say to her? A mother's tongue is sometimes worse than her hands.

MRS. DENHAM.

Yes, I know you think me a vulgar scold.

DENHAM.

I think you sometimes say more than you mean—more than you realise at the time. I wonder where the child has gone?

MRS. DENHAM.

Oh, she has slunk away to some of her friends. (*Throwing off the shawl, and letting her feet drop on the ground.*) Arthur, are you uneasy about her?

DENHAM.

Yes, rather. Jane heard her sobbing in her room, and saying she would run away.

MRS. DENHAM.

Why didn't you tell me that before? (*Rises, and moves to and fro.*) Oh, what have I done? What have I done?

DENHAM.

We must look for her. Some one may have seen her. Wait a moment. (*He opens the door, and meets Fitzgerald, who comes in smiling.*) Fitzgerald!

FITZGERALD.

(*coming down to back of sofa*) Well, I've brought you back your little waif, Mrs. Denham.

MRS. DENHAM.

Undine?

FITZGERALD.

Ay, Undine!

MRS. DENHAM.

Oh, I am so thankful! But where is she?

FITZGERALD.

Well, I left her below, having some milk or something. She seemed quite done up—excitement or something—eh?

DENHAM.

Where did you meet her, Fitz?

FITZGERALD.

I was going to my studio, and I met—met her running along the road with—with a little white scared face, and no hat on her—and her curls flying behind her—an'—an'—'pon my word, I could hardly stop her But we met a little girl with a goat, an' we stroked the goat—eh, stroked the goat—an' that comforted her a bit.

MRS. DENHAM.

But where was she going?

FITZGERALD.

Oh, that's the cream o' the joke! I had a great piece of work to get out of her what ailed her, an'—an'—would you believe it?—that Undine of yours—that Undine of yours was going back to her native element. The—the mite was looking for the Thames, to drown herself!

MRS. DENHAM.

To drown herself?

FITZGERALD.

Ay. She told me, "Mother said—said she was too wicked to live—an' she—she didn't want her any more." By Jove! Mrs. Denham, you must be careful what you say to that imp. She'll take you at your word—eh?

MRS. DENHAM.

How can we ever thank you, Mr. Fitzgerald?

DENHAM.

Well, we can laugh at it now; but it was rather a ghastly bit of tragi-comedy. A thousand thanks, Fitz, old fellow!

FITZGERALD.

Well, I hope she's none the worse for it. I carried her home on my back; an' I can tell you her heart was beating like—like the heart of a hunted mouse. I must be off, Arthur; I have a model coming. You'll bring the drawing round, eh? I must have it by five o'clock.

DENHAM.

I have about ten minutes' work on the background—the figures are all right. I'll bring it round just now.

FITZGERALD.

All right. Good-bye. (*Shakes hands, and exit.*)

DENHAM.

Stay here, Constance. I'll bring the child to you.
(*Exit, following Fitzgerald.*)

MRS. DENHAM.

Undine, my little Undine! Have I been a bad mother to you? And I have tried to do right. Oh, how I have tried! All in vain—all in vain.

(*Paces up and down, then sits listlessly on the sofa.*) Utter wreck! Utter wreck! Utter failure in everything!

(*Re-enter Denham, with Undine. Mrs. Denham starts up.*)

DENHAM.
Here's our little truant come back to mother.
(*Undine comes down the stage slowly, looking dazed. Mrs. Denham embraces the child passionately.*)

MRS. DENHAM.
My little Undine! My little girl! Did she think mother wanted to get rid of her?

UNDINE.
(*with sorrowful indignation*) You said you wished I was dead, and I thought you didn't want me any more. I thought perhaps you were going to kill me with a knife, like Medea, and I didn't like that. I thought the river would be kinder.

MRS. DENHAM.
That was foolish, Undine. Mother would not kill her own little girl.

(*Sits down on sofa with Undine. Denham shrugs his shoulders, and sits down at the table to work at his drawing.*)

UNDINE.
But I thought you meant what you said. You oughtn't to say what you don't mean, mother.

MRS. DENHAM.
No, my darling, I ought not. But I was angry with you for being disobedient, and I suppose I said more than I meant. I don't remember, Arthur, I don't remember what I said.

DENHAM.
I quite understand that, dear.

MRS. DENHAM.
Will my little girl forgive mother?

UNDINE.

Yes, you know I'll *always* forgive you, mother. But you said I had brought shame upon father. (*Going up to Denham, bursting into indignant tears.*) I don't *want* to bring shame upon father! (*Takes out her handkerchief, and mops her face.*)

DENHAM.

(*comforting her*) Of course not. But you know you should be obedient to mother, Undine, and keep your promises. Then we sha'n't be ashamed of our little girl.

UNDINE.

(*sobbing*) But there's no *use* promising. Oh, I *am* so tired! (*Yawns.*)

DENHAM.

Well, suppose you go to sleep for a while?

MRS. DENHAM.

She can lie on her bed, and I'll put mother's cloak over her. Would you like that?

UNDINE.

(*sleepily*) Yes.

(*Mrs. Denham leads her away, the handkerchief falls on the floor.*)

DENHAM.

(*gets up from the table, takes his pipe, lights it, and sits down again*) Everything seems torn up by the roots here. What is to become of that monkey? She has routed her mother, horse, foot, and dragoons, this time. Well, it's a wise mother that knows her own daughter. (*Works on again.*) Going to drown herself! Perhaps it would have been better if her father had hung himself long ago. There's always that question of: To be or not to be?
(*Re-enter Mrs. Denham.*)

MRS. DENHAM.

She's asleep, Arthur.

DENHAM.

Poor little ugly duck!

MRS. DENHAM.

I suppose you think I have acted very injudiciously?

DENHAM.

(*sighing*) Oh, what does it matter what I think? You always act on principle. I *must* try to get this drawing done.

MRS. DENHAM.

Don't send me away, Arthur. You will soon be rid of me altogether.

DENHAM.

Don't say that, dear. I know you are very miserable about Undine—and other things. So am I. I wonder whether we are all going mad.

MRS. DENHAM.

I think *I* have gone mad.

DENHAM.

Do you say that in earnest?

MRS. DENHAM.

You know there was—something in our family.

DENHAM.

Oh, nonsense, Constance! For Heaven's sake don't brood over that. There is something in every family, if one only inquires. Your nerves are over-strained. I wish you'd go to bed, and let me have some one to see you. You are looking like a ghost.

MRS. DENHAM.

I feel like one. But I am not going to haunt the scene of my crimes any longer. I am going away—going away!

DENHAM.

Well, I'm going with you, then, to take care of you. We'll send Undine somewhere, and go abroad for a while.

MRS. DENHAM.

Oh yes. You can be kind enough, if that were all.

DENHAM.

Will you never make peace?

MRS. DENHAM.

The only peace I *can* make.

DENHAM.

What do you mean?

MRS. DENHAM.

I shall trouble you no longer.

DENHAM.

My dear girl, don't talk like that. It is ghastly. Constance, I must go to Fitzgerald with this wretched drawing. I have to give some directions about the reproduction. I sha'n't be long. Promise me that you won't do anything foolish—that I shall find you here when I come back.

MRS. DENHAM.

Yes—you shall find me here.

DENHAM.

That's right. (*Goes to settee, and takes up shawl.*) And now lie down here, and let me cover you with this shawl.

MRS. DENHAM.

Very well. (*She lies down.*) Arthur!

DENHAM.

Yes, dear.

MRS. DENHAM.

Kiss me once before you go.

DENHAM.

Oh, if I may! (*Kisses her.*) My poor Constance! I would give my heart's blood to comfort you. And meanwhile I'll send you a better thing—tea.

MRS. DENHAM.

Thank you, dear. You have always tried to be good to me. You could not help being cruel, I suppose.

DENHAM.

I want to be good to you always. Well, good-bye, and God bless you! (*Kisses her.*)

MRS. DENHAM.

God bless you! (*Exit Denham.*)

MRS. DENHAM.

(*listens for a while, then starts up*) He had tears in his eyes when he kissed me. Poor Arthur! he thinks we are going to patch it up, I suppose. I am to live on pity—a man's pity, more akin to contempt than to love. Why *should* he love me? I was not born to be loved, not made to be loved. And yet I wanted love so much. I wanted all or nothing, and I have got pity—pity that puts you in a madhouse, and comfortably leaves you to rot! Oh, my God! is this madness—this horror of darkness that seems pressing on my brain? (*A knock at the door.*) What's that? Come in!

(*Enter Jane with tea.*)

No, not there, Jane—the small table; and bring another cup, will you?

JANE.

Yes, m'm.
(*Jane places tea-things, and exit.*)

MRS. DENHAM.

What have I to do? Ah, yes. (*Sits at the table and writes hurriedly. Re-enter Jane with a cup.*) Jane, take this note to Mrs. Tremaine's at once. You know the house?

JANE.

Yes, m'm.

MRS. DENHAM.

(*giving note*) Take it at once.

JANE.

Yes, m'm. Was I to wait for an answer, please?

MRS. DENHAM.

No, Jane; no answer. (*Exit Jane.*) She will be here directly. She *must* come—and I? Yes—yes. There is no other way of quitting the wreck for *me*. The key? (*Searches her pockets.*) Yes! (*She goes to the cupboard, opens it, and takes out a small bottle, places it on the tea-table, and looks at it; then takes out the stopper, and smells the poison.*) It smells like some terrible flower. (*Re-stops and replaces the bottle.*) And now to arrange—to arrange it all decently. (*Pushes the couch behind the screen, returns to the table, and pours out a cup of tea.*) My throat is parched. (*Drinks eagerly.*) Poor Arthur! He will be sorry—perhaps he will understand a little now. (*She pours the contents of the bottle into the cup.*) The Black Cat had a friend; I am not so fortunate. It is a survival of the fittest, I suppose. The world was made for the sleek and treacherous. (*She replaces the bottle in the cupboard, then returns, and lays the keys on the table.*) Yes, my little Undine, mother is tired too—so tired! Oh, sleep, sleep! If it were but eternal sleep—if I could be *sure* I should never wake again! No more life. And yet I want to live. Oh, my God, I want to live! (*Paces to and fro, mechanically putting things in order; sees Undine's handkerchief on the ground, and picks it up.*) Undine's little handkerchief, still wet with her tears—the last human thing on the brink of the abyss. Poor little rag; it will give me courage to face the darkness. (*Kisses it, and thrusts it into her bosom, then goes back to the table.*) Perhaps I *do* think too much of things—even of death. And now! (*Takes up the cup and shudders.*) Who said "Poor Constance"? (*Puts it down again, and presses her hands to her ears.*) There are voices in my brain—voices that burn like the flames of hell. Sleep, sleep—we must cheat the madness. (*Takes the cup, and passes* r, *as if to go behind screen.*) How awfully things look at you when you're going to die! I did not know this. There's Demeter with Undine's wreath of daisies withered on her head. My life has withered with them, since that day she made the libation. She forgot the speedwell for me. Mother! Mother! Mother! This is my libation! (*Drinks the poison, and lets the cup fall.*) It is done! (*She stands a moment perfectly still.*) My God! not sleep, but horror! Quick! Quick! (*Staggers behind the screen, and throws herself on the couch, where she is hidden from the audience.*) Arthur! Arthur! Oh! save me! Arthur—oh! (*Moans and dies.*)

(*A pause, then enter Denham and Mrs. Tremaine.*)

DENHAM.

Constance! I left her here on the sofa, and now—Constance! She must have gone to her room—she sometimes does. Have some tea, won't you?

(*They approach the tea-table.*)

MRS. TREMAINE.

I don't know why I have come here, I am sure. I never meant to see this place again; and yet, here I am, like the good-natured fool I always was.

(*He places a chair for her by the table.*)

DENHAM.

It was awfully good of you to come. That's such a strange letter for Constance to have written. She asked you to come here at once, for my sake and your own?

MRS. TREMAINE.

Yes. It's a mad kind of letter. (*She sits down.*)

DENHAM.

I am very uneasy about her.

MRS. TREMAINE.

Well, what's that to me?

DENHAM.

Nothing, of course. Blanche, we have been living in hell since yesterday.

MRS. TREMAINE.

I daresay. I have not been in Paradise, I assure you. What are you going to do? (*Pours out some tea.*)

DENHAM.

I don't know.

MRS. TREMAINE.

(*puts in sugar*) Will she—stay with you?

DENHAM.

What else can she do?

MRS. TREMAINE.

(*stirring her tea*) Then I wish you joy of the *ménage*. You don't seem to have gained much by making a fool of me.

DENHAM.

You have renewed the world for me. The mere thought of you is sunshine. Here we have always been at loggerheads with life.

MRS. TREMAINE.

Then why—? (*Sips her tea.*) Bah! Upon my word, Arthur Denham, that woman has drained you of your manhood like a vampire, made you the limp coward that you are.

DENHAM.

Not a word against Constance, or I shall hate you, Blanche. No—I am haunted by a ghost.

MRS. TREMAINE.

A metaphorical one?

DENHAM.

The ghost that came to Hamlet in the shape of his father—duty. It is a trick of my British bourgeois blood, I suppose.

MRS. TREMAINE.

What duty? To that internal Mrs. Grundy we call conscience? To the thing called Society? To the sacred bond of marriage? Her own principles are against you there. No—she holds you in some deeper way than this.

DENHAM.

It is true—she does.

MRS. TREMAINE.

(*rising*) Is it because you love *her* that you abandon *me*? If so, say so; and I shall understand that I am a toy goddess, nothing more.

DENHAM.

She loves me.

MRS. TREMAINE.

Ah! a woman's love can blight as terribly as a man's—almost. Well, I like you none the worse for this curious spice of loyalty. It is so rare in a man.

DENHAM.

No—not so rare. Don't let us talk any more about it now. I think you begin to understand. But where can she be? I seem to feel her presence here. (*He looks behind the screen, then thrusts it aside, showing Mrs. Denham lying dead on the couch.*) Blanche! Blanche! Look here! Is she—?

MRS. TREMAINE.

She has fainted—let me—!

DENHAM.

(*throws himself down beside the couch and puts his finger on her wrist*) Oh my God! Dead! Dead!

MRS. TREMAINE.

No, no, no! It is too terrible! Let us try if— (*Attempts to open dress, then recoils in horror.*) And I had begun to hate her—yes, to *hate* her. My poor good Constance!

DENHAM.

But how—? (*Rising.*) *Is* she dead, Blanche?

MRS. TREMAINE.

(*mastering her agitation*) Yes, dear, dead! She has taken poison. See here! (*Picks up the cup.*) What a horrible death! Her face is awful!

DENHAM.

Oh, Constance, why did I leave you? I had a vague fear of something—but not this! (*Throws himself down again, and stoops to kiss her.*) Ha! Prussic acid! No help! No hope! Yet she is warm. (*He starts up.*) Could we—? But death is a matter of seconds with that infernal stuff. Blanche, Blanche, I have killed her!

MRS. TREMAINE.

I claim my share in the guilt.

DENHAM.

No, no. Leave me! Let the dead bury their dead!

MRS. TREMAINE.

If you wish me to leave you, dear, I will go.

DENHAM.

Yes—for God's sake, go! (*She moves towards the door.*) But, Blanche, don't leave the house. I can't bear this alone.

MRS. TREMAINE.

(*returns to him*) You know, dear, I am yours always. Oh, don't hate me! I dare to say it in this presence. (*She kisses his hand. He shrinks from her.*) Now I can go. (*She goes to the door and looks back as Denham kneels and clasps the body in his arms.*) Will he hate me now? (*Exit Mrs. Tremaine.*)

DENHAM.

Constance! I meant to have kept you from all the thorns of life! It was fate! It was fate!

CURTAIN.

www.ingramcontent.com/pod-product-compliance
Lightning Source LLC
LaVergne TN
LVHW091204080426
835509LV00006B/827